Margaret Kerr

P. FIELD

Marlyn Sachtjen

Marcia

C. Miller

Louise

Geoffrey E. Beasley

Bill Sloop

Garcia

EX LIBRIS

Randy Manning

Mark Bramble

Worrell F Trimble

Eden
on Their
Minds

Eden on Their Minds

American Gardeners with Bold Visions

STARR OCKENGA

Clarkson Potter / Publishers
New York

Published by Clarkson Potter/Publishers, New York, New York.
Member of the Crown Publishing Group.

Random House, Inc. New York, Toronto, London, Sydney, Auckland
www.randomhouse.com

CLARKSON N. POTTER is a trademark and POTTER and colophon are registered trademarks of Random House, Inc.

Printed in China

Design by Helene Silverman

Library of Congress Cataloging-in-Publication Data
Ockenga, Starr.
    Eden on their minds: American gardeners with bold visions / by Starr Ockenga.—1st ed.
    1. Gardens—United States.   2. Landscape gardening—United States.   I. Title.
SB466.U6 O29   2001
712'.6'0973—dc21   2001021059

ISBN 0-609-60587-9

10 9 8 7 6 5 4 3 2 1

First Edition

FRONT JACKET: Bryan Garden; BACK JACKET: Trimble Garden, Reames Garden; Strohbeen and Luchsinger Garden, Bowell Garden, Cochran Garden; PAGE 1: Beasley Garden; FRONTISPIECE: Draney Garden; CONTENTS PAGE: Cochran Garden; PAGE 8: Kerr Garden; PAGE 9: Draney Garden; PAGES 10–11: Cochran Garden; PAGES 12–13: Homans Garden; PAGE 232: Blue Arch, sculpture by Anna Benes, Bryan Garden; PAGE 233: Bryan Garden; PAGE 234: Himalayan blue poppy (*Meconopsis grandis*), Homans Garden; PAGE 235: Homans Garden; PAGE 240: Bryan Garden.

To the memory of my father, Harold John Ockenga,
minister, orator, scholar, writer, photographer, and lover of the land,
and
to each of the gardeners in this book

The portrait of my father was made by John Ockenga, my brother, in the spring of 1968. When my father was a young man, he became the pastor of an active Boston church. It was a calling to which he was passionately dedicated. But he also had a private vision. For vacations he would take his young family to the mountains of New Hampshire for spiritual and physical refreshment. My parents bought a nineteenth-century farmhouse, at the end of a dirt road. The house, uninhabited for a decade, and the overgrown land that surrounded it needed work; my parents did it themselves over the following forty years. While my mother grew old-fashioned flowers—tansy, phlox, and daylilies—on a stone terrace, my father, in worn preaching shoes and a felt hat, worked in the fields and forests. He mowed the pastures with a scythe, and he planted hundreds of saplings. Our land was his garden. Each morning at first light and again at day's end, my father, seated on his favorite bench under an old pine tree, read the Bible. In that quiet place he lifted his eyes to the hills and the sky and gave thanks to his god.

Contents

Introduction

*"Do not go where the path may lead,
Go instead where there is no path—and leave a trail."*
—Ralph Waldo Emerson

They work and create outside the mainstream. They push conventions and boundaries. They make their own rules, and break them with confidence. Unafraid to take risks, they follow their own instincts. They define new directions. They inspire. Visionaries and mavericks, these gardeners are making a dynamic, lasting impression on the American landscape.

While the styles of these innovators are ever changing, like quicksilver, there are some common threads.

Fundamental to each gardener's philosophy is a deep concern for the land and an awareness of the increasing fragility of the larger environment and of the endangerment of specific plant species. Louise Smith has spent a half a century rescuing Alabama's native plants from encroaching development, and Marlyn Sachtjen restored a midwestern prairie while reforesting portions of her land. William Woys Weaver in Pennsylvania represents a burgeoning movement dedicated to collecting, preserving, and growing heirloom plants — in his case, vegetables.

Parallel to this sensitivity to the limits of our land is a resolve to make gardens that blend with the natural landscape, allowing the wild and the cultivated to overlap seamlessly. Many of these gardeners repeat phrases like "listening to the land" and "fusing the garden with the site." Karen Strohbeen and Bill Luchsinger formed grand, undulating garden beds in response to the shapes of the Iowa landscape. Mary Homans carved a woodland and alpine garden featuring both native and exotic plants out of a rocky hillside, marrying it so closely with the greater Maine landscape that the garden appears to have been growing in place forever.

Mary is also a model for the practice of integrating house and garden into a unified whole. At her California-style house a flight of wide steps leads to oversize glass doors. When duplicated on the opposite side of the house, these doors allow a view through the building and across terraces to the rocky coast of the Atlantic Ocean beyond.

These gardeners are sophisticated in their knowledge and use of gardening traditions in American history and around the world. Their approaches allow them to adapt foreign design concepts, mix them with American customs, add personal touches, and create something fresh and unorthodox. A suggestion of Sissinghurst lingers at Afton Villa, but as Genevieve Trimble said, "We borrowed from England, interpreted the Louisiana gardening tradition, and made this garden into our own modern version of a garden in ruins."

Sarah Draney, deeply moved by centuries-old remnants in the Irish landscape, hints at ancient mysteries in the haunting contemporary sculpture garden she has created in upstate New York, and Jack Miller looks to the Japanese gardening traditions, even as he encourages Pennsylvania native mosses to blanket his hillside.

While conventionally pretty beds and borders in muted hues still have a place in the American gardening consciousness, many of these gardeners have a weakness for wildly colorful giants, imports from the tropics. Tenderness, then, is no longer taboo. For Sonny Garcia and Tom Valva, the primary criterion for plant selection in their San Francisco garden is

striking foliage color. Linda Cochran seeks audacious plants for her garden that will survive northwestern winters, and Michael Bowell, a determined zone basher with jungle fever, has converted his Pennsylvania plot into a fantasy land of tropical splendor.

Many of these gardens are not really about flowers. Woody plants are now receiving their just due, and not only as the backbone of gardens, as in the living walls that divide Geoffrey Beasley's Oregon garden rooms or in the majestic old specimens that line Neville and John Bryan's broad allées in Illinois. For some, trees and shrubs are a garden's most prominent features. Justin Harper has dedicated a quarter of a century to growing fine

conifers; these plants *are* his Illinois garden. Richard Reames merges the lines between tree collector and tree sculptor by planting living chairs and houses in the Oregon landscape. This *is* the time of the tree.

Artists-gardeners are creating works specifically for the garden; again, ancient and modern traditions provide inspiration, yet the works are boldly original. Marcia Donahue nods to the South Sea Islands, but with a twist, as she carves stone into evocative heads or oversize persimmons or peaches in her Berkeley garden. Margaret Kerr pays homage to Middle Eastern tribal carpets in the brick rugs that dot her Long Island landscape. A spirit of playfulness, of letting things take shape spontaneously, drives many toward charming results. Karen Strohbeen and Bill Luchsinger make whimsically rustic support structures for their plants, and Richard Reames uses saplings to fashion a peace symbol or a heart against the sky.

Rather than collecting everything—and, of course, few can resist a strange plant with brown flowers that is a challenge to grow—a number of these gardeners have become focused on a singular idea or plant. While Mark Bramble collects a diverse range of plants in

his New York City indoor garden, orchids have become his passion, and Dino Anagnost, in a magnificent gesture, dedicates an entire Hudson Valley field to growing every variety of sunflower he can order from the dozens of catalogs that land on his kitchen table. For Paul Held, even a single genus—the primula—was not a narrow enough theme; he became entranced by *Primula sieboldii,* and he obsessively collects and propagates this winsome flower in his Connecticut woodland garden. The lure of breeding plants drives Justin

Harper to develop new dwarf conifers, and Bill Radler, Milwaukee's man of a thousand roses, to hybridize superior low-maintenance roses.

Gardeners are by nature generous; more and more are opening their gates to the public. Visiting private gardens has become a national pastime and a resource for the dissemination of new ideas to the larger gardening audience, in great part because of the Garden Conservancy's initiation of its Open Days Program a decade ago. Gardeners like Geoffrey Beasley and Jim Sampson now host their own events, often inviting hundreds of people to benefit favorite projects and charities.

Volunteerism in creating and caring for green spaces in public areas is a mission to which a number of gardeners have dedicated their efforts. Louise Smith, for example, with a small group of other women, spearheaded the creation of the Kaul Wildflower Garden at the Birmingham Botanic Garden. Justin Harper, a horticultural philanthropist, has twice

donated the entire contents of his garden to arboretums in the Midwest in order to establish conifer collections.

When I began this search for boldly conceived and boldly executed gardens I thought I was on a hunt for the work of an esoteric minority. I soon realized that vast numbers of gardeners were creating their own unique, brave worlds.

The twenty-one gardens described here, all very different from one another, are thrilling examples of the extraordinary range and brilliance of private gardening in America today. They—and all the like-minded gardening adventurers—are making our country the most exciting place in the world to be a gardener at the beginning of this twenty-first century.

Starr Ockenga
Livingston, New York

Karen Strohbeen

"We make the rules, and then we break them. Isn't it fun?"

Bill Belsgo

garden, designed and lovingly cared for by the owners, grew by the side of the house. "I like it," Bill said. Karen agreed.

The couple, both successful artists, had sought a location where their passion for gardening could flourish, where, as Bill says, they could grow older and never move again. They spent portions of each year in Brooklyn, New York, as many-up-and-coming artists do. But, Iowans by birth and temperament, they eventually returned to their home state, settling for the first few years in the western part of the state.

They had met at Drake University's art school in Des Moines. Karen and Bill came from gardening backgrounds, and both cite their grandfathers as influences. Gardening became an increasingly powerful force in their lives. A deep connection exists between the imagery on the walls of their house and the garden pictures framed by its windows: prints, sculptures, ceramics, drawings, paintings, videos, and an ambitious perennial garden.

ABOVE: **A 12-foot-wide, 300-foot-long mown path runs parallel to the pond; it crosses the dam and leads to the wildflower meadow. Karen and Bill travel extensively visiting and filming gardens across America and in Europe for their PBS television series.**

"For me," muses Karen, "gardening is making art outdoors. All the same principles apply."

Working together, Karen and Bill, who have made pieces of sculpture with a joint signature, accumulated plants, expertise, and equipment. The Winterset place came with 80 acres of rich farmland that answered their need for expansion. For the first five years they maintained, and enjoyed, the existing herb garden "out of respect," as Karen recalls. Gradually, however, their ideas for experimentation dictated changes, and they embarked on an innovative plant study program. They removed the original brick paths and in their place installed

fifty-four 4-foot-square raised boxes made of treated pine 4-by-4's spaced 2 feet apart. "We never plant anything we plan to eat in boxes made of treated lumber," Bill observes. "This garden is strictly for testing perennials."

Karen divides the growing season—and the location of beds—into four color-coded demarcations: late winter to early spring—blue; late spring to early summer—green; summer—yellow; and fall—red. Karen never plants two summer boxes or two fall boxes adjacent to each other in the Box Garden. Using a mathematical system devised by Bill, Karen organizes the arrangement so that one season's box flows into the next, creating a colorful patchwork pattern throughout the grid. Always the artist, she insists that the experimental nature of this garden not detract from its beauty or limit its color combinations. She says, "We are thinking about time, space, color, line, texture, making pictures within the 4-foot frames." In each bed Karen tests a group of plants with similar cultural needs and overlapping bloom periods. Just as significant, however, is how well each plant gets along with its bedfellows.

Karen thinks about the size that each mature plant will demand aboveground. For example, a low-mounding plant and a tall, narrow plant do not inhabit the same air space and can be planted quite close to each other without becoming crowded. The plant's habit underground, she stresses, is just as important. A plant with a long taproot can occupy approximately the same space as one with a shallow root clump.

Karen admits, "I am looking for exciting plant combinations." While a box might primarily contain summer-performing perennials, she might also insert spring-flowering plants, like Oriental poppies. The box would have a splash of electric orange or salmon pink in spring, and the foliage of the summer bloomers would camouflage the hole left by the poppies as they go dormant.

Certain categories of plants automatically take assigned positions, as on an athletic team. Grasses go into autumn boxes, where they provide interest all summer, before peaking and blooming in the fall. Conifers are planted in the late-winter and early-spring boxes, as they

LEFT AND BELOW: In designing beds, Karen says, "I want to create a layered effect with each plant combination. Then I try to achieve a visual weaving of one bed into another, a sense that the foreground is merging into the more distant parts of the garden, including the pond, and, finally, into the land beyond." BELOW LEFT: A Japanese tree lilac (*Syringa reticulata*) presides over the entrance to the House Beds;

its arching branches give the effect of an oversized arbor. Karen often uses the strong vertical punctuation of a tree, whether deciduous or conifer, to define a transition between one garden and another. OPPOSITE: In the Box Garden, Karen and Bill put plant combinations through a rigorous testing program before bringing them out into the main gardens. For each bed, a grid of tracing paper is attached to a piece of cardboard, one sheet for each season. By flipping the tissue layers Karen and Bill can see each season's layout at a glance. A basic grid formula, which Karen follows when planting the Box Garden, ensures that no two seasons' beds are adjacent to each other.

TOWERING BEAUTY

Rustic Structures

"STRUCTURES ARE as important as plants to the look of this garden. I used to try to hide them, but since we need to have them in the garden to provide height and architecture, we decided that they might as well be beautiful," says Karen of the twenty-five rustic *tuteurs,*

Since red cedar (*Juniperus virginiana*) grows wild in local hedgerows and fields, Karen and Bill use it as the primary material for creating structures in their garden. "It's a great material," says Bill. "It is easily accessible and springs up in profusion; we are only thinning out crowded areas when we cut it. It generally grows very straight, and it will last for years."

He insists that most "household pruning can be used in making ornamentation for the garden. Use whatever sources you have. Grapevines, which grow wild and often strangle a host tree, make wonderful building material. You are doing yourself and the environment a favor by putting these vines to good use."

Often, after they make a structure out of cedar, preferably spring-cut for maximum flexibility, Karen and Bill will embellish the sides or top with willow curlicues. "Willow is easy to twist into swirls and curls, but it lasts only a couple of years before it must be replaced," Karen observes.

The structures are built on a square base of ⅜-inch plywood with 4-inch carriage bolts inserted from the underside. The dimensions, which are arbitrary, depend on the size desired for the bottom of the *tuteur.*

or tripods, that stand throughout the garden.

Each bed has several *tuteurs,* varying in height from 3 to 14 feet and in shape from short, wide, and rounded to tall, thin, and pyramidal. "We design the shape and height of the structures around a plant's growing habit," Karen says. *Clematis recta* 'Purpurea', a naturally spherical plant, fills a 3-foot dome, while a dozen vase-shaped *Clematis* × *durandii* become columns of deep blue-purple blossoms.

For a 12-foot *tuteur,* Bill might put the screws about 30 inches apart. He adds, "For a five-sided structure, like the shorter mounded ones, I place five screws at equal distances around a circular shape on the plywood."

Meanwhile, Karen chooses cedar saplings of fairly uniform length. She clips branches off the sides but often leaves the tops intact, stripping needles from some and leaving needles on others. The wispy branches can add interest to the top of a completed structure. She coils the topmost branches into decorative shapes, securing them with wire.

Once the saplings have been evened off at the bottom Karen selects three metal Grow-Thrus, circles of open wire mesh, in decreasing sizes—24, 20, and 16 inches—which give plants additional support. Working together Karen and Bill wire the saplings to the bolts on the base with 17-gauge electric-fence wire, which does not rust. (The base will ultimately be removed when the *tuteur* can stand alone.) Once secured at the base, the saplings are joined at the top; then the Grow-Thrus are wired in place at even intervals.

"Now comes the fun part," says Karen. "I can play with the design." She chooses smaller cedar saplings or branches with forks or twists of growth. "Cedar is really flexible when fresh," she notes. When they are affixed around the sides starting a few inches from the ground, they offer diagonal support, without which the tripod would collapse. "Remember, clematis and other perennial woody vines are heavy plants. When covered with a mature *Clematis* × *jackmanii,* there is serious wind stress on the tripod. Whimsical twists and circles of the cedar make the finishing touches at the top," explains Karen. "Perching birds go crazy for this part. All these tripods are homes to birds."

To install the tripod, Bill drives three rebar stakes 12 to 18 inches into the ground and wires them in two places to the legs of the tripod. The legs of the tripod are not buried: their feet rest on the ground, so the bottom of the tripod legs will not rot faster than the rest.

Delighting in the effect of these picturesque structures, Karen and Bill have not limited themselves to building *tuteurs.* Garden fences and rustic rooms are also made of the long-lasting material. A pavilion complete with window-like openings makes a discreet enclosure outside their dining room window. The walls are papered with the fast-growing sweet autumn clematis (*Clematis terniflora*). Bird feeders filled with thistle are hung in the openings, and a dozen yellow finches often join the couple for dinner.

TOP: **Even though different gardens have different color schemes, when the gardens' beds are just across a path, Karen echoes certain colors, like the purples of salvias and irises on the left and** *Nepeta* **'Blue Wonder' on the right. Mirroring certain hues ensures harmonious transitions from garden to garden.** ABOVE: **The delicate and fragrant** *Lilium pumilum* **(often sold as** *L. tenuifolium***) in massed groupings adds accents of orange throughout the early summer.**

provide form and structure when the rest of the garden sleeps and as it wakens in the spring.

When a combination pleases the couple, it is ready to debut in the main garden, a series of grandly proportioned island beds that occupy the 200-foot slope between the buildings and the pond. "I would never suggest that people create island beds," says Bill. "Generally, they don't complement suburban settings, where they are so often used. But here they seem to repeat the contours of the surrounding landscape. Their shapes were our response to what we see when we lift our eyes."

The half-dozen beds cover 2 acres, curving around one another, like embracing lovers. Each island is raised 2 feet higher along its entire central axis; this additional height gives the bed a startling new dimension, and drainage is dramatically improved.

Iowa is known for its excellent soil, which is often referred to as black gold. Bill reports that 25 percent of the world's Class A soil is in Iowa. However, because it is so rich and fine, compaction and drainage can be problematic. Therefore, in preparing the soil for a new garden, a program that takes a year, Karen and Bill always use the same formula: one-third garden soil, one-third coarse sand, and one-third organic matter such as manure or compost, all of which Bill tills together until well mixed.

Removing the stump of a dead tree triggered plans for the House Beds. Bill proposed three irregularly shaped beds nested within one another and enveloping the south end of the house.

earth is an advertisement for t
soil once a year by spreading a

The only other soil cover u
box gardens are softened with
materials, and sawdust is som
quiet, almost contemplative."
Encroaching grass is given cri
revealed earth. Plants don't l
sive, narrow border of rosy s
perpetual challenge.

Floribunda and English roses offer fragrance and a long season of bloom. *Clematis* × *durandii* with abundant purple-blue flowers thrive in congregations of rustic *tuteurs,* some as tall as 14 feet. Blue spruce (*Picea pungens* 'Glauca Globosa') on standards, positioned like oversize lollipops, add a touch of humor. The beds are underplanted with spring bulbs and alliums, especially *A.* 'Globemaster', selected because its dying foliage is less offensive than that of some of its relatives.

The Lily Garden—named for its array of Asiatic, regale, Oriental, and species lilies—fills two beds that lie back to back. Plants, in their varied forms, can be architecture. "But they are not enough," says Karen, "especially in winter and early spring." Conifers and grasses add texture and height in a garden with no physical walls. A staggered line of Alberta spruce trees

A separation between the Lily Garden and the Cool Summer Garden opens to a panorama of the pond. Karen says that the use of positive and negative spaces is integral to the design of each garden area. "The sizes and shapes of the grassy pathways, which position you to perceive the gardens, are just as important as the forms of the beds. My father

When designing a gar
"Think about being able
wide paths in the Box G
Plants that require the n
ent plants and spring-fl
Karen cut back perenni
tection in a winter with
dropping to minus 30°

In recognition of th
Perennial Gardener with

"We are trying to sh
nitty-gritty, we hope t
we visit are dirt garde

(*Picea glauca* 'Conica'), with their pointed caps, march through the bed, providing contrast to balls of arborvitae (*Thuja occidentalis* 'Hetz Midget') or *Pinus strobus* 'Nana'.

Since all these island beds are expansive in scale—one is 25 by 75 feet—Karen and Bill have created a system of narrow dirt paths that are hidden from view. One rule is cast in stone: they never step directly on the prepared earth. If they have to walk into a planted area, they first place a small board a little bigger than a work boot on the ground and step on it.

Bill says, "The plants are our mulch. They provide a cover that is cool and clean and low in maintenance." And indeed very little soil is visible. In the rare spot where it can be seen, the

was an engineer who studied patterns of walking. He determined that people naturally walk in spirals. They cut a corner tightly, and then ease the curve as they walk a distance. We kept those principles in mind as we created the bed and path shapes."

A PIONEER'S PATH

Louise Goodall Smith
Birmingham, Alabama

WHILE HER contemporaries were creating gardens influenced by the great lawns and long borders of England, Louise Smith has been blazing a different trail, both philosophically and physically. Over the last half century, this remarkable woman has often been just one step ahead of the machines as they moved phalanx-like across Alabama, creating highways and dams, clear-cutting the timberland, and destroying the habitats of many native plants. Here come the bulldozers, the backhoes, the cranes. Here come the men in hard hats carrying sticks of dynamite. And here comes a lady with a trowel. Weezie Smith, the Florence Nightingale of plants, is here to save the trilliums. A woman of great determination, she resolved to rescue native plants and to make a refuge for them on her own property. In time, she would make gardens, both personal and

Louise Goodall Smith

"The challenge was twofold: not only saving native plants but learning about growing them."

public, that maintained the spirit and conditions of the deciduous woodlands in the wild.

"When I began, I knew absolutely nothing about gardening. Nothing. I'd never seen a hepatica, nor did I know a hexastylis," she says, laughing. The stories of her rescue efforts are legion. When Clear Creek Falls, a magnificent waterfall "that was the prettiest spot in the state, where local families gathered to picnic" was slated to be engulfed by Lewis Smith Dam, Weezie scooped up hemlock babies; three are mature trees in her garden today. When a congressman broke ground for a lake excavation, Weezie dashed 80 miles to the site and dug up galax and *Trillium catesbaei*. At a site of new construction near her home, a brush hog was grinding a stand of royal ferns to a pulp. "I was able to save one little frond. It took a long time to recover," she says ruefully.

Alabama has four major geographical areas, each very different from the others: the Coastal Plain, which extends to the Piedmont; the Ridge and Valley area; the Cumberland Plateau; and the Highland Rim in northwest Alabama. Thus the state is endowed with great biodiversity. Weezie reflects, "The sad thing is that Alabama is fifth on the list of states that have the greatest number of endangered species (after California, Florida, Texas, Hawaii)." She does not view her dedication as exceptional, claiming, "It seemed like the most natural thing to do. In the beginning I was really ambitious, I wanted to collect every ornamental Alabama native. I had to give up on that idea, but over the years I've acquired many of them."

At first Weezie brought nothing more with her than missionary zeal, a topographical map, and a compass; by the 1970s, having exhausted a series of station wagons, she purchased a four-wheel-drive International Harvester Scout to help her reach difficult terrain. "I spent at least one day a week in the woods and considerable other time at construction sites," she remembers. Often her children went with her. "I could go anywhere I wanted, do anything I wanted, as long as I took five children along." Determined to educate herself, she took classes—one each quarter for seven years – in subjects like geology, physics, and organic chemistry. Eventually she became an authority on southeastern native plants.

Weezie worked tirelessly to preserve the habitats of endangered species. She has served as an expert witness in the legislature on issues concerning land conservation, ecology, and preservation. She participated in a two-year botanical study, including a collection of herbarium specimens, of Sipsey Wilderness in the Bankhead National Forest for the United States Congress.

In the 1960s Weezie joined forces with Barbara Orr Kaul, Margaret Wimberly, and Susan Kinnear, and together they spearheaded the effort to found the Kaul Wildflower Garden, endowed by Barbara Kaul and her husband, Hugh. Located at the Birmingham Botanic Garden in the remains of a spectacular pink sandstone quarry, which was used in the 1930s by

PREVIOUS PAGES: **Louise Smith's signature plant, the wild blue phlox (*P. divaricata*), blankets her property, weaving amongst azaleas and ferns, with a lavender-blue haze in April. The cutting garden is bisected by a gravel path leading to a greenhouse. Even in Birmingham's Zone 8A climate, winters can be cold, with temperatures sometimes dropping to**

zero. Weezie commissioned a simple underground sun pit made of cement block with the walls below grade. Inside, the temperature never dips below 40°F all winter. THIS PAGE, ABOVE: *Silene virginica.*

ABOVE: **The red of *Silene virginica* makes a stunning contrast to the blue phlox on Weezie's wildflower hillside.** RIGHT: **As Weezie cleared each section of her woodland, she covered it with two feet of leaves, supplied by the city at her request in the fall. After the area rested for a couple of years, she planted rescued wildflowers, like *Trillium decumbens,* which has colonized throughout the garden.** OPPOSITE: **The slope of Weezie's woodland varies from a gradual incline to a steep 45-degree angle. Paths wind in broad curves, and sets of steps, made of aged and moss-covered railroad ties, access the steeper inclines.**

the WPA, it is sliced down the middle by a rushing stream. According to Gary G. Gerlach, the garden's director, "Weezie was the plant authority, and she knew the taxonomy." Although the other founders are now deceased, new volunteers have joined the effort. They share Weezie's determination to maintain and continue to develop the renowned garden.

Weezie reminds us that all this happened over almost five decades. "One step at a time," she modestly says, brushing off a reputation that has made her a household name across the South. Weezie's story started traditionally, even inauspiciously. In 1950, Weezie, then a young mother, and her husband, Lindsay, an accountant, purchased four acres of land outside Birmingham in a residential area called Mountain Brook. The Smiths, who were apartment-bound, craved the outdoors for themselves and their growing family. It was five years before they could build their house. A low contemporary structure on a southeast-facing hillside, it opens to the surrounding woodland, which was thick with tulip poplar, oak, hickory, beech, and dogwood trees. They moved into their new home in March of 1955 with two toddlers and one baby in a basket; twins would arrive shortly.

Weezie recalls that the land was smothered in vines: poison ivy, Japanese honeysuckle, and

catbrier or smilax. "First we had to remove four hundred dead pines, and then the vines. It happened gradually." But from the beginning Weezie had a vision of repopulating her land with Alabama natives.

The property's neutral to slightly acidic loam is hospitable to rhododendrons, azaleas, mountain laurel, and many of the ephemeral spring wildflowers, like trilliums. Weezie says she has found that plants known to prefer alkaline conditions, like wild blue phlox and trout lilies, will adjust to acid soil, whereas those that are found in acid soil, like the fleeting pink lady's slipper, refuse to convert. The same one-way formula applies to plants whose natural habitats are wet or dry: those plants that prefer wet feet will often adjust to dry conditions, but plants that like dry conditions will die if their roots stay wet.

The Smith garden has always had demarcation lines that, while strict in concept, seem nat-

BELOW: "When I started to make a garden, the only way to get a native azalea was to dig it up and carry it. Native azaleas like this *Rhododendron austrinum*—in white, pink, orange, and red—are so much more ethereal than their oriental cousins," Weezie says of their open growing, arching habits. "They are very promiscuous, and are still evolving in the wild, as well as their hybrid counterparts in nurseries." Azaleas require an acid soil. Because there is such a broad range of varieties, the sequence of bloom begins in March and follows through July.

ural in execution. Transitions between the gardens are seamless. Above the house, which is set on a plateau in the middle of the property, the woodland hillside is divided by the driveway. The area is designated exclusively for native plants. Below the house, the garden is terraced by retaining walls, which Weezie built by hand. The "city plants"—camellias, wisteria, hellebores, tulips, African daisies, and daffodils—are arranged in a rather formal pattern. The separation seems invisible, but the rules are absolute: the natives may wander at will into the city plants' domain, but the reverse is strictly forbidden. Native plant habitats are sacred and are not to be invaded by exotics.

Spring in Weezie's garden is a glorious season. The tall tree canopy has not yet leafed out, and the light flickers across the hillside as though touched by the tip of a magic wand. The delicately perfumed flowers of native azaleas in white, pink, and gold hover over the garden, like clouds of butterflies. The spring ephemerals—those plants that appear, flower, and then disappear for the rest of the season—densely carpet the hillside. Trout lilies (*Erythronium rostratum, E. umbilicatum,* and *E. americanum* var. *harperi*), resembling little golden bells, arrive first, with the snow-white bloodroot (*Sanguinaria canadensis*) not far behind. Then the wild blue phlox (*P. divaricata*) envelops the entire garden with a shimmering cloud of pale blue and lavender. Pockets of white rue anemone and star chickweed glow like handfuls of pearls strewn upon the earth. The gray-blues of camassia, Jacob's ladder, and amsonia are a soft backup chorus.

The thrilling trilliums—at least twenty-three varieties—number in the thousands. They often take five to seven years from seed to bloom, which makes them one of the most elusive and coveted of the spring ephemeral plant families. Their flowers range from the mysterious greens, reds, yellows, and browns of *T. cuneatum, T. decumbens,* or *T. underwoodii* to the nodding white of *T. flexipes* and the otherworldly pink of *T. catesbaei.* Some, like *T. luteum* and *T. sessile,* have spotted foliage that looks like heartshaped pieces of marble tossed on the forest floor.

Weezie says she has often been asked, "'When spring is over, what do you have?' A quieter garden, to be sure," she admits, "but there are the spigelias (*S. marilandica*), the hypericums, the oak leaf hydrangeas, and the ferns," of which Weezie grows at least thirty different varieties.

"If you rescue five plants, you have five hundred if you stay long enough in one place," she says of the plants that have colonized by the thousands. "I'm a good digger. I'll tackle just about anything."

Weezie says one ingredient in her recipe for success has been to bare-root all her plants, from the tiniest rue anemone to shrubs and trees. When she brings a plant to her garden, she shakes the soil off its roots, washes it, and then plants it in its new home and waters it well. She does this, she points out, in the spring and fall, not in the heat of summer. Weezie believes that plants acclimate to her soil better if they do not carry any part of previous homes, which may be incompatible with her own soil.

She also recycles all plant debris. Her compost bins are located behind a fence, along with a nursery where plants are nurtured before heading to the main gardens. Because of the heavy leaf fall, the garden does not lack for mulch. Weezie's system is to use the fallen leaves for winter protection. She removes them—by hand and in buckets—in early spring. She then grinds them in a shredder and puts the mulch back in the garden, an extremely time-consuming task that she cannot always accomplish throughout the entire garden. When the old leaves remain, spring ephemerals are slower to appear.

Weezie starts her day with a walk in the garden in her robe, coffee in hand. She assesses the garden's needs and decides on the order in which she will address them. Then she dons her uniform of black jeans and boots and begins. "All I do is work," she says, of the eight to ten hours she spends in the garden each day. "And I love it. I like doing it more than I care about seeing the results. If I get good results, that's my bonus."

ABOVE: **Weezie calls a sunken courtyard beside her house the City Garden. She designed it to have a formal structure, outlining a central rectangle with brick paths. In spring, when the daffodils and tulips make their show, the garden also seems to have walls of pink and white rhododendrons. As in all of Weezie's gardens, the wild blue phlox seed themselves with glorious abandon.**

Trout lily (Erythronium americanum v. harperi)

THE WILD ONES

Louise Smith's Spring Wildflowers

WEEZIE DUG most of her woodland wildflowers in the wild, but she notes that these days it is illegal to dig many of these plants, particularly those that are endangered. Instead, she advises purchasing plants from reputable nurseries. Look for plants that are listed as "nursery-propagated," not "nursery-grown," which may mean that the plant has been dug up from the wild but kept in a nursery bed for a short period.

These plants are called spring ephemerals, because many disappear altogether, including their foliage, during the summer months, then return for another delicious spring.

Their natural habitat is the deciduous forest, where the spring sunlight filters through the trees' bare branches and a heavy leaf canopy offers protection from the heat and summer sun. Most prefer neutral to slightly acid soil; using the leaves (preferably shredded) as mulch adds richness to the soil.

BOTANICAL NAME	COMMON NAME	FLOWER COLOR	HEIGHT
Amsonia ciliata	Blue milkweed, bluestar	Periwinkle blue in panicles	1–3 feet
Amsonia hubrectii		Sky blue in panicles	To 3 feet
Amsonia tabernaemontana	Bluestar	Pale blue in panicles	2 feet
Anemone quinquefolia		White, tinged with pink	10–20 inches
Anemonella thalictroides	Rue anemone	White, cup-shaped	4 inches
Aquilegia canadensis	Wild red columbine	Red and yellow nodding flower	20–30 inches
Arisaema dracontium	Green dragon	Slender green	12–18 inches
Arisaema triphyllum	Jack-in-the-pulpit	Pale green, purple markings	12–18 inches
Baptisia alba		Slender racemes of white	To 3 feet
Baptisia australis	False blue indigo	Slender racemes of dark blue flower	To 3 feet
Baptisia bracteata	White false indigo	Slender racemes of cream-white flowers	To 3 feet
Camassia scilloides	Wild hyacinth	Violet, gray-blue, white racemes	18 inches
Claytonia virginica	Spring beauty	White, pink-tinged	12 inches
Coreopsis auriculata	Coreopsis	Bright yellow, solitary	10 inches
Cypripedium calceolus	Yellow lady's slipper orchid	Yellow	16 inches
Cypripedium kentuckiense	Yellow lady's slipper orchid	Yellow	16 inches
Delphinium alabamicum	Alabama delphinium	Electric blue or purple	To 3 feet
Delphinium tricorne	Dwarf delphinium	Blue, violet, or variegated with white	To 3 feet
Dentaria diphylla	Two-leafed toothwort	White	6–8 inches
Dentaria laciniata	Cutleaf toothwort	White, four-petaled, flushed with pink or lavender	6–8 inches
Dicentra cucullaria	Dutchman's breeches	White, clustered	9–12 inches
Dodecatheon meadia	Shooting star	White	16 inches
Erythronium albidum	White trout lily	White, solitary, nodding	6 inches
Erythronium americanum var. *harperi*	Yellow trout lily	Yellow, tinged with brown, solitary, nodding	6–9 inches
Erythronium rostratum	Yellow trout lily	Yellow, solitary, nodding	6 inches
Erythronium umbilicatum	Yellow trout lily	Yellow, solitary, nodding	6 inches
Galax urceolata	Galax, wand flower	White	8 inches
Geranium maculatum	Wild geranium, cranesbill	Pink, white, lavender clusters	1–2 feet
Hepatica acutiloba	Liverleaf	Bluish or white	4 inches
Hepatica americana	Round-leaf hepatica, liverleaf	Lavender-blue to white	4 inches
Heuchera americana	Alumroot	Greenish yellow to purple lacy clusters on stalk	18 inches
Heuchera villosa	Hairy alumroot	Greenish yellow to purple lacy clusters on stalk	18 inches
Iris brevicaulis		Deep blue to purple blue	18 inches
Iris cristata	Dwarf iris, crested iris	Pale blue to deep blue	6 inches
Iris verna	Vernal iris	Violet-blue to white	6 inches

ABOVE: *Trillium catesbaei*
LEFT: **Bloodroot** (*Sanguinaria canadensis*)
RIGHT: *Trillium rugelii*

Strawbell (*Uvularia perfoliata*)

Isopyrum biternatum	Isopyrum, false rue anemone	White in clusters	5–6 inches
Jeffersonia diphylla	Twinleaf	White, cup-shaped	6 inches
Mertensia virginica	Virginia bluebells	Sky-blue to purple-blue	18 inches
Phacelia bipinnatifida	Spotted phacelia	Violet-blue in loose clusters(biennial)	1–2 feet
Phacelia purshii	Miami mist	Pale blue, white center	To 2 feet
Phlox divaricata	Blue woodland phlox, wild blue phlox	Blue to lavender, white	8–18 inches
Phlox stolonifera (white form)	Creeping phlox	White	6 inches
Polemonium reptans	Jacob's ladder	Lavender-blue	9–12 inches
Polygonatum biflorum	Solomon's seal	Pale green to white bells, hanging in pairs under leaves	2–3 feet
Sanguinaria canadensis	Bloodroot	White	6 inches
Shortia galacifolia	Oconee bells	White	6 inches
Silene polypetala	Fringed pink	Pink	1–2 feet
Silene virginica	Fire pink, scarlet catchfly	Red	1–2 feet
Smilacina racemosa	Smilacina, false Solomon's seal	White in tiny clusters	14 inches
Stellaria pubera	Star chickweed	White	8 inches
Stylophorum diphyllum	Celandine poppy	Yellow to orange	1 foot
Tiarella cordifolia var. *collina*	Foam flower	White, pinkish	9 inches
Tradescantia virginiana	Virginia spiderwort	Blue to lavender	2 feet
Trillium catesbaei	Catesby's trillium	Pink	8–10 inches
Trillium cuneatum	Whippoorwill flower	Brown, yellow, green	12–18 inches
Trillium decumbens		Brown, yellow	6 inches
Trillium flexipes		White	12 inches
Trillium luteum	Yellow trillium	Yellow	10 inches
Trillium pusillum	Least trillium	White, turning to pink	4–8 inches
Trillium rugelii	Nodding trillium	White	12–15 inches
Uvularia perfoliata	Strawbell	Pale yellow	18 inches
Zephyranthes atamasco	Atamasco lily	White, trumpet-shaped	8–15 inches

Coreopsis (*Coreopsis auriculata*)

Trillium flexipes

Zephyranthes atamasco

MASTER OF ILLUSION

Mark Bramble
New York City

HIGH ABOVE Manhattan's busy streets, Mark Bramble tends to the demands of some five hundred plants. There, atop one of the city's oldest apartment buildings, the Osborne, Mark has created a sumptuous indoor garden. When the elevator reaches the eleventh floor, it opens onto a foyer, where a spectacle of seasonal plants, from spring bulbs to white poinsettias, bask under a 14-foot skylight. The arrangement is just a preview of what waits behind Mark's door.

In his refuge Mark mixes his love for the theater and his passion for plants, especially orchids. This Broadway playwright is no stranger to dramatic gestures; on a recent birthday, he released a dozen butterflies among the orchids to the applause of celebrating guests. An ebony baby grand is encircled by a hundred myrtle topiaries, and eighteenth-century theatrical figures stand amid lacy fern foliage.

Mark Bramble

"When I go into my Orchid Room, I enter another state of awareness."

A wall of theater posters and awards forms a colorful backdrop for pots of orange poppies, pink and white hyacinths, and a speckled orchid (*Degarmoara* 'Flying High') that appears to be costumed in animal skin. French wire plant stands, garden benches, statues, and ornaments are the props that make this urban space feel like the formal garden of a country house. "A tableau in every room" is Mark's motto.

Bold statements have always come naturally to Mark. While a young student at Boston's Emerson College he wrote to David Merrick and told him, "I will come to work for you for free, if you'll teach me the theater." Mr. Merrick ultimately produced two of Mark's plays, *42nd Street* and *Barnum,* which opened within five months of each other in 1980. "It was a pretty heady time," Mark recalls.

After a ten year sojourn in London, as the director of *42nd Street,* Mark returned to New York and purchased the south- and east-facing apartment in the Osborne sight unseen. Taking a walk one afternoon in his neighborhood, Mark passed the garden shop of the New York Horticulture Society. He bought six African violets and gave them a home on his bedroom windowsill. "London is famous for its pastoral pleasures. It has so many parks that one never feels deprived there," Mark says. "In New York we live in closer quarters. The hankering for green, for bringing the outdoors indoors, got the best of me." Sweeping his arms in a gesture of incredulity at the plants on every available surface, he observes, "The rest is history."

The original half-dozen violets burgeoned to more than a hundred. Mark joined the African Violet Society, a turning point that he recalls as an intense learning experience. The group is serious and scientific, yet practical. "Studying the habits of one genus teaches you much about growing others," he notes. He trained himself to keep meticulous notes on the feeding and nurturing of violets, a discipline he maintains for all his plants.

Rather than a collection of plants clustered under lights or strung out in a police-station line-up, Mark was determined to create a series of cohesive gardens, environments conducive to plant health and aesthetics. He says the success of indoor gardening depends on four major considerations: ventilation, humidity, light, and temperature. These are the keys to plant health—and to the avoidance of frustration for the gardener. In each of his gardens these matters are the first ones he addresses. He asks himself, What does each plant family require?

He started by taking advantage of the apartment's limited natural light. He installed 12-inch glass shelves in all the deep-set windows. The easily removable shelves provide flexibility both for cleaning and for 3-foot plants to take their turns at the windows. With natural light in short supply, Mark by necessity began experimenting with artificial light. On this subject, he says, indoor gardeners express an endless stream of controversial opinions. "The only right answer is what works for you, and that can only be determined by experimenting."

PREVIOUS PAGES, LEFT: **A fountain in Mark Bramble's bedroom garden is surrounded by orchids, including** *Phalaenopsis, Degarmoara, Brassolaeliocattelya,* **three** *Cattleyas,* **and an** *Ondontoglossum.* RIGHT: **Amongst a collection of myrtle topiaries, Mark adds white poinsettias, amaryllis, and various forced bulbs for the holiday season.** THIS PAGE, ABOVE: **A vignette of hyacinths, narcissi, ranunculus, and amaryllis are arranged beneath an office wall of theater memorabilia.**

BELOW: **An 8-foot-tall plant stand in the kitchen has four shelves lit by Verilux tubes, which provide the two ends of the light spectrum that plants need: the red end for foliage and the blue for flowering. The shelves are ventilated by clip-on fans. This tableau: Iceland poppies, 'Tête-à-tête' daffodils, myrtle, hyacinth, lady's slipper orchids, and the pert orange** *Dendrobium*

Mark's living room garden is in constant flux, like a stage where performers set up for a limited run. A tiered plant stand holds a display of evergreens, the backbone of an indoor garden. Mop-headed myrtles, solenostemon, *Tradescantia discolor,* lavender, *Helichrysum, Plumeria,* ferns like the hare's-foot (*Polypodium aureum*) or *Asplenium antiquum, Eugenia,* Chinese evergreen (*Aglaonema* 'Silver Queen'), the ponytail plant (*Beaucarnea recurvata*), and black mondo grass (*Ophiopogon planiscapus* 'Nigrescens') are joined by transient soloists in bloom. All, whether star or supporting actor, sway, as though to the sounds of backstage music. In reality they are moved by the gentle breezes from 36-inch fans.

One garden occupies an entire side of Mark's bedroom and includes more than one hundred plants. "This is the Madagascar garden," Mark says matter-of-factly, as though every urban apartment has one. After reading an article in *Orchid Review* about the climate preferred

cuthbertsonii. **Mark now grows over twenty-five different orchid species, including** *Angraecum, Cattleya, Dendrobium, Laelio-cattleya,* **the jewel orchid (***Ludisia***), the lady's slipper orchid (***Paphiopedilum***), and the Mandarin orchid (***Phragmipedium***).**

by the pitcher plants and numerous orchid species, Mark decided to duplicate the South Seas climate and create his own tropical oasis.

Framing the bedroom garden, a trompe l'oeil wall of age-cracked sandstone mimes the proscenium of a Broadway stage. Chiseled into the lintel is the date 1996. The theatrical surround, constructed of two-by-fours and plywood, camouflages an elaborate lighting system, which evolved over five years. Mark says, "I began with a design based on the principle of a lighting grid, like the one a rock band would use at Madison Square Garden." The structure, modified in scale to fit his bedroom, holds twenty 8-foot alternating cool and warm fluores-

cent strips, installed both vertically and horizontally, and twenty-four 4-foot strips across the ceiling. As the 60-watt fluorescent bulbs burn out, Mark is replacing them with Verilux full-spectrum tubes, which he considers superior. He is also doing this in all of the artificially lit gardens in his apartment. Positioning the lights on the back side of the surround has the effect of making the plants, which lean toward light, face their audience. The lighting rig also holds three tracks that carry 50-watt, 12-volt halogen spots, used solely as decorative lighting. When guests arrive, the fluorescent bulbs are turned off, and the garden seems to be illuminated by invisible light sources.

On the floor, three 4-foot-square galvanized tin pans hold creek rock, pebbles readily available from nurseries. Before the pans were set in place, Mark lined the floor with industrial-weight plastic, both to catch drips and to keep condensation from destroying the parquet floor. He maintains a half-inch of water in the pans to elevate the room's humidity. Mark tries to push the humidity level up to 50 percent in each room at least once every day to combat the habitual dryness of apartment climates. "New York apartments are generally kept at about 20 percent humidity—drier than the Sahara Desert," he says.

While Mark's plants appear in picture-perfect health, he notes that intensive indoor gardening takes vigilant policing. Bathing plant foliage is one solution to the pest problems that are inevitable with indoor gardens, and ventilation and humidity are the best deterrents. But when pests do invade, Mark calls his own personal army of "good bugs" to the rescue, as he believes in biological pest control. In his refrigerator next to neat rows of hyacinths receiving their twelve-week cold period stand containers of sleeping bugs.

"Perhaps the most persistent pests in indoor gardens are the mealybugs, the matinee ladies of white hair and fur coats." They prefer myrtle, solenostemon, African violets, streptocarpus, and orchid foliage. Mealybug destroyers (*Cryptolaemus montrouzieri*) are sprinkled sparingly, like hot pepper flakes, over the plagued plant. Aphids, too, rarely rest. "They adore the little crocuses and tulips," Mark says. His aphid warriors are the red-uniformed ladybugs (*Hippodamia convergens*), which arrive in colonies of 1,500, packaged in plastic bags. Every ten days or two weeks, Mark takes a handful—he estimates about three hundred—and places them on a saucer with a little water. Removed from the refrigerator, they wake up from their chilly sleep and go industriously about their business: eating. Mark keeps a magnifying glass, outfitted with a light, for seeking out tiny spider mites. Their microscopic predators are packaged in plastic bottles filled with sawdust. He sprinkles a mixture of three of these predators (*Phytoseiulus persimilis, Neoseiulus californicus, Mesoseiulus longipes*) over an ailing plant.

ABOVE, FROM TOP: *Cattleya* **hybrid;** *Dendrobium aggregatum.* **For those making their first foray into orchid culture, Mark recommends starting with the "easy orchids,"** *Dendrobium, Catasetum, Cochleanthes, Pathiopedilum, Phalaenopsis, Phragmipedium,* **and** *Oncidium.* OVERLEAF LEFT: **Shelves display varieties of solenastemon.** RIGHT: *Phragmipedium grande* **'Macrochilum'.**

Whitefly parasites (*Encarsia formosa*), adhered to perforated cards, are hung from an afflicted plant's foliage at two-week intervals for about four applications. Fungus gnats are controlled by microscopic predator nematodes (*Heterorhabditis* and *Steinernema* species). Sold by the millions, they are applied by diluting their package with water and feeding it to the besieged plant.

Whether penning musicals or designing gardens, Mark plans details for theatrical effect. He tinkers, changes, and moves furniture, ornaments, and props, on the pages of a script and in the apartment. His workday is balanced between garden tasks and editing on the computer screen. "Half of my time to each task," he says. While his garden is a year-round job, he observes that the indoor gardener dances to a different seasonal rhythm. Fall, for him, might be called spring to others, as his paper-whites come into bloom in mid-October. Winter is the big-splash season, with the waxy-petaled, sweetly scented *Angraecum* orchids performing their spectacular number just in time for the holidays. "They give such pleasure," Mark says.

ORCHIDS
The Bramble Method

ORCHIDS, the prima donnas of the indoor garden, demand special conditions, so Mark Bramble has converted a bathroom into a habitat that he calls the Orchid Room. Here he has built shelves, put up rods for hanging plants, and installed lights and an automatic humidifier. A ceiling fan that runs twenty-four hours a day and a half-dozen clip-on fans from the hardware store keep the air moving constantly. This little room, just 7 by 10 feet, efficiently houses more than two hundred orchids, plus a few other pampered pets.

Phragmipedium besseae

The iron shelves, designed with lipped edges, contain a layer of creek rock and half an inch to one inch of water. A built-in system drains off excess water back to the bathtub. The walls are painted in a sunny yellow marine paint to prevent mildew.

Three kinds of light, set on eighteen-hour timers, illuminate the Orchid Room. Mark concedes that the brilliance, which seems to ricochet off the walls, is not easy on the eyes. The main sources are high-intensity sodium and metal halide. The sodium provides the red end of the spectrum, advantageous for bloom, and the metal halide promotes green growth. Forty-watt Verilux tubes stretch across the shelves, supplying light in areas obscured from the main system.

Because the room is small, Mark is able to push the humidity to 100 percent once a day; he sometimes runs the shower "as hot as it will go" for a half hour, along with the humidifier, which is always set at 70 percent. Orchids require a day-to-night differential of at least 10°—"and 15 to 20° is ideal"—particularly while they are setting buds, to bloom properly. The small space means that Mark has difficulty getting the temperature low enough even by leaving the window open, except on the most frigid nights. Daytime temperatures hover around 80°F, and the temperature rarely drops below 62°F, which occurs at night when the lights are off. *Masdevallias* and the pansy orchids (*Miltonia* and *Miltoniopsis*), which require periods of even lower temperatures to bloom, are kept closest to the open window to take full advantage of the cold air.

The inhabitants of the Orchid Room are carefully monitored. "Orchids thrive on a high standard of hygienics—they don't like dirt." Containers, which range from slatted wood baskets to square terra-cotta melon pots from Provence, are scrupulously cleaned before use. Drainage is critical; water is never left sitting in a pot except for the *Phragmipediums,* whose pots are set in bowls of clear water that is changed at least once a week.

Mark says he is constantly experimenting with planting mediums. *Paphiopedilums* "can be happy in lava rocks for a few years," and he uses a mixture of two-thirds lava rock and one-third charcoal, with a top dressing of New Zealand sphagnum moss. Most of the rest need to be repotted once a year. Roots are carefully cleaned of rot, and babies are separated from the parent plant and given their own pots. For *Phragmipediums* Mark mixes one part medium bark, one part tree fern fiber, and one part sphagnum moss; for *Phalaenopsis,* two parts medium bark, one part sphagnum moss, and one part charcoal. For a general mix he recommends two parts medium cedar bark, one part lava rock, and one part sphagnum moss. Mark uses the constant feed method, giving the orchids a 1-to-4 dilution of balanced 20-20-20 fertilizer with every watering.

Brassolaeliocattleya Hawaiian Passion 'Carmelia'

Asconfinetia hybrid

Paphiopedilum hybrid (*P. chamberlainianum* var. *liemianum*
'Halls' × 'Helen')

Brassia hybrid

A MODERN PLEASURE PALACE

Geoffrey E. Beasley
Portland, Oregon

GEOFFREY BEASLEY has built a mansion of many rooms, but, unlike those constructed of brick and mortar, his is formed from living trees and shrubs. Infused with a spirit of fantasy, wonder, and whimsy, this vast series of enclosures, romantically called Bella Madrona, has evolved into a contemporary pleasure garden.

Long corridors with 12-foot-high walls of tightly woven beech, hornbeam, and hemlock connect the seemingly countless spaces, each with its own distinct character. Some have evocative names: the Moon Garden, Ruby's Sunset Garden, the Etruscan Slope, the Belvedere, the Past Garden, the Crocodile Path, and the Fish Grotto. Twisting stone stairways invite exploration. Tiki torches border narrow paths and broad avenues while a multi-colored banner flaps in the branches of a Douglas fir and a huge

Geoffrey E. Beasley

"Walls of green create spaces filled with suspense and surprise."

aluminum pinwheel sends reflected light bouncing across the garden. A stage, outlined in velvety yew, sits above a ballroom where a group called Pink Martini recently played for five hundred revelers who danced the night away on the grand and grassy floor.

Geof and his partner, Jim Sampson, are hosts par excellence and they believe their garden's beauty is for sharing. "We are both southerners," observes Geof, "and we love to entertain." They open the garden frequently to their friends and to the larger Portland art, dance, and political communities.

In 1980, Geof and Jim, both doctors, moved to Portland from Arizona. Geof practices general medicine at the Portland Veterans Administration Hospital, and Jim, a clinical research physician, specializes in AIDS work. In Portland the men found a more varied climate, closer proximity to the ocean, and "an interesting cultural atmosphere."

They immediately went house hunting, heading for the Willamette River valley south of Portland, where open farmland with rich soil could still be found. When the men first saw the 1892 house in the foothills of Parrett Mountain, it was "just a dinky little farmhouse," but it came with five acres of land, Douglas firs, dozens of elegant cinnamon-barked madrones (*Arbutus menziesii*), and a hundred-year-old lilac in a graceful pastoral setting.

Through two renovations the little house has doubled in size. The men reversed the orientation of the house so that it now faces the gardens. The conversions, designed by architect John Forsgren, resulted in a two-story living room, an open kitchen, tall windows and French doors, a porch with a hot tub, and walls to showcase the owners' extensive modern art collection. An open deck atop the bedrooms provides a panoramic bird's-eye view over the valley and garden.

Because of the inevitable encroachment of suburbia, the first priority was to establish a buffer zone of hedgerows around the property. Over the years, dense plantings have completely encircled the gardens, like ancient castle walls enclosing a complex of structures. A dozen giant sequoias (*Sequoiadendron giganteum*) spaced on 6-foot centers were planted across the front of the house. Washington hawthorns, Portugal laurels, Lombardy poplars, native incense cedars (*Calocedrus decurrens*), and mixed groupings of viburnum, ilex, pyracantha, weigela, and climbing roses thickly outline other sections. The thick vegetation insures privacy and muffles the sound from the increasingly busy road. "It is a whole different world when you enter the driveway," Geof reflects.

Geof is the gardener; he does all the design and maintenance in the garden himself. Jim is the appreciative audience and a wise sounding board, often making suggestions about the

PREVIOUS PAGES, LEFT: **The Winter Garden is underplanted with heath, heather, and hebe, some of which flower during the overcast months from November to March. The floor is a mosaic in gold, silver, green, copper, and brown.** RIGHT: **An**

arched doorway in a wall of European beech (*Fagus sylvatica* 'Rohanii') opens to Ruby's Moon Garden, where mass plantings of *Ligularia dentata* 'Desdemona', *Persicaria amplexicaulis* 'Atrosanguineum', and *Fuchsia magellanica*, threaten to engulf the paths. THIS PAGE, ABOVE: **The multilayered bark of the garden's namesake tree, Madroño (*Arbutus mensiesii*).**

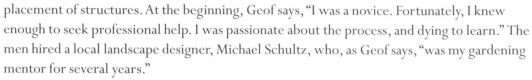

placement of structures. At the beginning, Geof says, "I was a novice. Fortunately, I knew enough to seek professional help. I was passionate about the process, and dying to learn." The men hired a local landscape designer, Michael Schultz, who, as Geof says, "was my gardening mentor for several years."

The bones of the garden, many of which were established in those first years, hark back to ancient traditions: from walled medieval herb gardens to terraced Italian hillsides, from outdoor Greek amphitheaters to Islamic rills of water and trickling fountains or Asian temples with carved stone guardians stationed at their entrances. Enclosures vary in size from 10 feet square to the Great Lawn, which measures 100 by 75 feet. Those closest to the house are rectilinear in shape, often with axial lines running through them. "Formal structure

BELOW: **In the Winter Garden, the deep green of** *Chamaecyparis thyoïdes* **'Red Star' contrasts with** *Chamaecyparis pisifera* **'Lemon Thread' in a living wall.** RIGHT: **At the entrance to the 25-by-100-foot Winter Garden, the open structure of** *Ulmus parvifolia* **'Yatsabura' contrasts with**

the densely needled *Chamaecyparis thyoïdes* **'Little Jamie' and a carpet of** *Calluna vulgaris* **'Robert Chapman'. Ornaments, sometimes bought but often found, like the sculptural sheers and rolls of wire placed on a stone column, make reference to Japanese gardening imagery, but with an individualistic American twist.** RIGHT: **A long, twisting gravel pathway leads through the Winter Garden. The focal point at the far end is an inviting wooden bench, placed in front of a 15-foot-high living wall of** *Juniperus scopulorum* **'Moonglow'.**

gives license to ebullient planting. The first complements the second," Geof observes.

The mixed borders, some 15 feet deep, have varied color schemes. While the combinations vary from soft gray and pastels through vibrant orange and bronze to a garden Geof describes as "wildly red," he says it's important to select a repertoire of shrubs that retain their shape and texture throughout the seasons. "Flower color comes and goes, but a great deal of color can be had in the foliage of well-chosen shrubs." For a soft fountain shape, Geof favors weigela, particularly the dark foliage of *W.* 'Wine and Roses' and the variegated green and gold of *W. praecox* 'Variegata'; the silver-gray *Buddleia alternifolia* 'Argentea'; a smoky blue-gray dwarf Arctic willow (*Salix purpurea* 'Nana'); the lacy gray of sea buckthorn (*Hippophaë rhamnoïdes*); and *Acnistus australis,* a borderline hardy volcano of blue bells covering gray foliage. For smaller mounded shapes, he uses the tight, glossy green of *Spiraea* × *bumalda* 'Crispa', *Physocarpus opulifolius* 'Diablo', and boxwood. Columnar choices include *Buxus sempervirens* 'Graham Blandy', arborvitae, or Italian cypress.

Geof also seeks out plants with winter interest. To provide lively color and texture during the cold months, he uses conifers, boxwood, ilex, and broad-leafed evergreens, like coast silk tassel shrub *Garrya elliptica* 'James Roof' or 'Evie', *Neolitsea sericea* with its golden silky new growth, and a number of different oaks—Mexican oak (*Quercus mexicana*), Ubame oak (*Q. phillyreoïdes*), and huckleberry oak (*Q. vaccinifolia*).

During the summer months Geof works about thirty hours a week in the garden. "I'm usually working on twenty or thirty projects at a time. I'm really efficient and can go through this garden at a headlong pace." He notes, "My style of gardening is totally intuitive. Working is like going into a meditative state and just letting my muscles perform the actual labor. The garden seems to tell me what to do next, without my really thinking about it." He has of necessity developed some time-saving methods. The deep borders, for example, have secondary paths known only to Geof, which allow him to tend to hard-to-reach plants. Debris is never carried out of the garden; Geof spreads it on those hidden paths, where it breaks down and becomes compost. Hose heads have been installed throughout the garden, allowing Geof to water efficiently. In the early days, quantities of manure were added, as were other soil

TOP: **Geof accents the garden with tender, exotic plants,** like eucomis, many of which live year-round in pots. He points out that potted plants are the musical chairs of garden design. They are often moved around the garden to areas that need quick jolts of color, and then are easily transferred to the greenhouse for protection over the winter months. ABOVE: The "gorgeous gunnera," *G. manicata,* with its great sharply toothed foliage that can reach six or eight feet is marginal in Portland's climate. It is too large to dig up each year; to protect it for the winter, Geof cuts it back, mulches it heavily, and "hopes."

amendments, like rock phosphate, green sand, kelp meal, and fish emulsion, so his soil remains rich and productive. Now, if he thoroughly breaks up the soil before he plants, he rarely feels the need to feed his plants. "Once in, they are on their own," he says.

Geof favors big, tropical-looking plants. Early on he discovered a considerable range of candidates—from bananas, gingers, and cannas to palms—that would thrive in his Zone 8 climate. "I'm always pushing the envelope, and I lose some, but I wanted this garden to have an exotic feel," Geof explains. "This is basically a Mediterranean climate, just a bit cooler, so we can also grow plants from Chile, South Africa, Australia, and New Zealand." A few essentials must be coddled, like the huge-leafed Chilean native gunneras whose crowns Geof covers in the winter. Geof points to an *Echium fastuosum* 'Pride of Madeira', a native of Spain. Bursting from the gray foliage are enormous blue spires. Though not reliably hardy, it is generous with its seedlings, which Geof transplants out of the gravel walkway into pots for winter safekeeping.

As Geof's penchant for the exotic grew, more tender plants crept in. To overwinter the

TOP: **To add more textural interest and color, Geof encourages vines, like the greenish-white flowering cup-and-saucer vine (***Cobaea scandens*** 'Alba') to climb through his living walls.** ABOVE: **Amongst the densely planted borders are single bold accents, like glazed urns, gazing balls in bright reds or blues, or a thoughtfully placed banana with huge burgundy foliage. These staccato spots of color, Geof believes, arrest the viewer's eye from its slower passage along the dense plantings.**

new brood, a greenhouse became a necessity; one was added in 1982 to the backstage complex of nursery, cold frames, and equipment shed. Abutilons, brugmansias, red cordylines, and a purple-veined, velvety-leafed *Solanum quitoense* must be dug out of the ground, cut back, and sent for a winter rest under glass. Potted plants, including eucomis, cacti, and other succulents will join them to wait out the cold weather.

Geof admits to being an accumulator not only of plants but also of the flotsam and jetsam of modern life. "I collect everything," he says. "I've been known to come to a screeching halt on the highway to pick up a piece of twisted steel." Sculpture, fountains, and sundials are made of found objects, while broken gazing balls, hunks of metal, architectural fragments, and stained-glass windows add ambiguity to the garden. "I like the hint that something was here before, that deterioration has gone on. The place appears to have an enigmatic history."

Works by a number of contemporary artists and sculptors are also installed throughout the garden. Two stone heads by Marcia Donahue that seem to symbolize every man of every race lie side by side in the fishpond. Rusted metal ribs, suggesting the remnants of a ship or even a buried dinosaur, were installed by Douglas Wallower. Abstract iron gates and finials by Bradley Horn also serve a practical purpose, like keeping Hoss, the ancient pet horse, a

Garden ornaments—the non-plant part of a garden—can be "the stuff of intrigue," Geof says as he muses on the unique personality of his garden. "I gravitate to things that are unexpected, puzzling, unexplainable. I don't want the viewer to be able to read the garden and come up with an answer. I'd like to think that some questions are left open-ended. And therefore, the visitor's mind will retain an image for a long time. When questions are answered, we don't really care about them any longer, do we?" CLOCKWISE FROM UPPER LEFT: In Ruby's Moon Garden, a window in a beech hedge offers a small but evocative view out into the world beyond. A pair of well-worn garden chairs are placed facing away from each other. "Perhaps, they suggest a relationship or conversation that we'd like to know more about," Geof comments. A series of architectural gateways, isolated on a hillside path, are a memorial to a friend, George Payne, who passed away in 1989. The sounds and reflections of water add an otherworldly dimension to a garden, Geof says. By taking a group of unrelated found objects and assembling them into an abstract fountain, Geof created a sculpture that seems to have been plucked from a garden in outer space. Geof relates plants and objects by repeating or contrasting their forms, textures, or colors, as the hard surface of this concrete ball echoes the velvety gray of the licorice plant, *Helichrysum petiolare*. At the fern-shaded edge of a path, an inscrutable moss-covered Buddha holds a chunk of amethyst in his hands.

remnant of "our farm animal stage," in his fenced pasture. "The spirit of this garden is a product of the many people who have had a part in it and by those who are memorialized in it," observes Geof. "My favorite great-aunt is the Ruby of Ruby's Sunset Garden; I named it for her when she passed away at age ninety-seven. We have lost friends to AIDS, and their memorials are around the garden."

At the lower end of the more established gardens, the Etruscan Walk, edged with columnar Italian cypress, leads down the side of a hill into a topographical cup. The gentle incline with a flat grassy bottom is an ideal natural site for a small outdoor theater. Geof is developing his dream to host performance art in the space. He would also like to begin a garden school, using the master-apprentice model.

"I would teach the first, and the first would instruct the second. That way we would spread the knowledge, the great experience of working in the garden. To me making a garden is the greatest human creative act. It is a hands-on pass-along process of learning and understanding and tremendous satisfaction."

RIGHT: **Because of the orientation of a garden house, a double-arched and clouded window glows from within with afternoon sunlight. In a strangely unexpected juxtaposition of the world seeming inside out, the window reflects a garden on the other side of the building. But if one is inside the little structure, which is sparely furnished with simple wood benches and a table as in a meditation room, the same sensation occurs. The building is artfully draped with the deep-green leaves of an old grapevine and the contrasting yellow foliage of** *Choisya ternata* **'Sundance'.** OPPOSITE: **Walking through a beech archway from a larger garden room to a smaller one elicits a powerful feeling of transition. It is like leaving a long, public hallway and entering a private bed chamber; one feels the quiet, peaceful intimacy of this enclosed garden.**

LIVING WALLS
Tapestries in Shades of Green

LIKE A CALLIGRAPHER with a broad-tipped pen, Geoffrey Beasley draws bold lines across his land. These crisply defined strokes have become the framework of the garden's corridors and passageways, forming the exterior walls of tiny chambers and defining grand garden rooms.

First, Geof roughly outlines a shape he wishes to enclose. Then, using stakes and string, he refines the dimensions to precise architectural proportions—90-degree angles for corners, perfect curves for rounded spaces, or axial lines a prescribed number of feet apart. "Hedges will be in place a long time. It is essential to

hedge, creating a shimmering tapestry effect. For a 12-foot-high wall that separates the ballroom from the Moon Garden, he wove three varieties of hornbeam: purple hornbeam (*Carpinus betulus* 'Purpurea'), oak leaf hornbeam (*C. betulus* 'Quercifolia'), and *C. betulus* 'Fastigiata'. In the Winter Garden he mixed deep green conifers with golden-tipped ones. Sometimes in a sumptuous gesture he mixes deciduous and evergreen plants, as at the edges of the Belvedere where forsythia, bupleurum, *Thuja occidentalis* 'Sunkist', osmanthus, and mock orange entwine.

Geof lays out each plant before he picks up his shovel. He sets beech and hornbeam 2 to 3 feet on center. But he advises, "Know the mature girth of the tree, and space plants accordingly." Once laid out, he digs each plant's hole individually. When planting any woody plant—and Geof has planted thousands, counting the hedges—he digs a circular hole twice as big around as the plant's root ball, breaks the soil up underneath, and plants "gently." Then he uses a spade to break up all the adjacent soil for a foot or so around the circle, making the ground hospitable to the growing roots of the new plant. By berming up the soil around the plant, he provides a reservoir for retaining water.

An entrance in a tapestry hedge of three varieties of hornbeam leads to the Moon Garden.

get the placement correct. These walls are permanent separations between gardens, and they form backgrounds for plants."

To create doorways and large arched windows, Geof uses iron forms for support. For these he trains and shapes the plants as they grow, ultimately joining the tops and tying them together. Smaller windows and high clerestory apertures begin as small holes; as the plants grow Geof removes branches to make the opening larger. For a more window-like effect he leaves some of the branches in place to represent mullions.

Sometimes, Geof mixes more than one plant in a

"Clipping hedges is a labor-intensive occupation," Geof admits. He routinely climbs a 10-foot stepladder and, when necessary, a 17-foot orchard ladder. He rarely uses electric clippers, preferring hand tools, primarily hedge shears, sharpened frequently with a file. "But I often grab handfuls of foliage and cut them with my Felcos. This close-in clipping gives a more informal result." Some hedges, like Canadian hemlock (*Tsuga canadensis*) or *Taxus* × *media* 'Hicksii' must be sheared twice a year (in mid-May and mid-August), and hornbeam, three times, adding an additional midwinter haircut. "Bless the arborvitae," he says, as it does not need clipping.

BOTANICAL NAME	COMMON NAME	DESCRIPTION
Berberis thunbergii var. *atropurpurea* 'Rose Glow'	Barberry	New growth rose-pink mottled with deep purple; deciduous
Bupleurum fruticosum		Glossy blue-green foliage; early summer chartreuse umbels; narrow, upright; evergreen
Buxus sempervirens 'Graham Blandy'	Boxwood	Narrow, upright; evergreen
Carpinus betulus 'Fastigiata'	European hornbeam	Oval shape; fan-ribbed branches; does not develop a central leader; deciduous
Carpinus betulus 'Purpurea'	European hornbeam	New foliage is purple but fades to green as season progresses; deciduous
Carpinus betulus 'Quercifolia'	European hornbeam	Foliage is oak-like in shape; deciduous
Chamaecyparis obtusa 'Crippsii'	Hinoki false cypress	Broad pyramid; rich golden yellow tips on foliage; evergreen
Chamaecyparis pisifera 'Lemon Thread'	Thread-leafed cypress	Bright golden foliage; evergreen
Chamaecyparis thyoïdes 'Red Star'	False cypress	Conical, compact; bright green foliage in summer, turning reddish plum in winter; evergreen
Fagus sylvatica 'Rohanii'	Purple European beech	Deep purple foliage that holds its color into the summer; keeps crinkled brown leaves through the winter; deciduous
Forsythia 'Fiesta'	Variegated forsythia	Strong, upright yellow stems; yellow-centered foliage; yellow bell-like flowers in spring; deciduous
Ilex aquifolium var. *angustata*	Holly	Dark lustrous foliage; evergreen
Osmanthus heterophyllus 'Purpureus'	Purple false holly	Deep purple new foliage growth; small, fragrant white flowers in fall; dense bushy habit; evergreen
Philadelphus coronarius 'Aureus'	Golden mock orange	Bright golden foliage; fragrant white flowers in summer; deciduous
Picea likiangensis 'Purpurea'	Yunnan spruce	Deep green needles; evergreen
Taxus × *media* 'Hicksii'	Columnar yew	Narrow, columnar; lustrous dark green needles; evergreen
Thuja occidentalis 'de Groot Spire'	Eastern (American) arborvitae	Narrow, columnar; evergreen
Thuja occidentalis 'Emerald'	Eastern (American) arborvitae	Lustrous emerald-green foliage; does not discolor in winter; evergreen
Thuja occidentalis 'Sunkist'	Golden arborvitae	Bright gold needles; semidwarf; broadly pyramidal; evergreen
Tsuga canadensis	Canadian (Eastern) hemlock	Glossy dark green needles, lighter green in spring; makes a very tight hedge; evergreen

The Winter Garden walls are woven with many colors of conifers.

SINGULAR VISION

Paul Held
Westport, Connecticut

PAUL HELD claims he has fallen "blindingly in love" just twice in his life. He offered his heart first to a "lovely redhead," only to be smitten soon afterward with a tiny flower, the *Primula sieboldii*. "To both," he says, an impish grin creasing his otherwise reserved face, "I remain passionately devoted."

Today, more than twenty years later, Paul has the largest collection of *Primula sieboldii,* which he prefers to call by its original Japanese name, Sakurasoh, in America, with more than 550 varieties. Some 200 of them are named Japanese forms, which he has collected from Japanese devotees through persistent letter writing, seed and rhizome exchanges, and his travels; the remaining 350 are his own selections.

Paul married his sweetheart, Jane Sherman, in 1980. Jane

P. HELD

"My mission is to bring this special plant to the public's attention."

PREVIOUS PAGES, LEFT AND RIGHT: **Masses of flowering dogwoods, rhododendrons, azaleas, and variegated hostas are but staging for the stars of Paul Held's woodland garden,** *Primula sieboldii.* **Its original Japanese name, Sakurasoh,**

comes from the words for cherry blossom (Sakura) and for herb (soh). THIS PAGE, ABOVE: *Rhododendron* 'Hershey's Red' and the fragrant lilac flowers of *Daphne genkwa* are a bold backdrop for the delicately colored and diminutive primulas.

inherited a 2-acre parcel of wooded property in Westport, where she had begun to build a contemporary house. Together the pair completed their home, an open, gracious dwelling suited to their casual lifestyle.

Paul began to make a garden as a gift to his wife, who requested he "keep it kind of woodsy." The land, north-facing, sloped and rocky, was dense with ash and oak trees and tangled with poison ivy and honeysuckle. Paul, a middle-school fine arts teacher, cleared it section by section, working long hours on weekends and during his ten-week summer vacations. He determined to shape a garden that would enhance the inherent characteristics of the woodland and preserve native plants like trillium and jack-in-the-pulpit.

While he had never gardened before, Paul is a scholar by nature. He studied plant families that would thrive in his environment, and he was drawn to alpine varieties. Fortunately, a local nursery specialized in fine selections. He added gingers, hostas, ferns, rhododendrons, and azaleas that have flourished in the slightly acid soil. In retrospect he realizes he was setting the scene for enchantment. The real magic was yet to come.

On their first vacation together Jane and Paul made a pilgrimage to New Hampshire, where Jane's late great-aunt Audrey Townsend had been a devout gardener. Wandering the garden, Paul encountered a cluster of *Primula sieboldii*—delicate cupped primroses, pink on the outside and white within, nodding above a bouquet of crinkled leaves. Paul would not be parted from the beguiling plant; he dug up a clump and carried it back to Connecticut.

When Paul planted this New Hampshire seductress, however, it sulked and refused to set seed. At a loss, Paul joined plant societies. At that time the American Primrose Society did not offer *Primula sieboldii* in its seed exchange, but the Scottish Rock Garden Club and the Alpine Garden Society of England did, and he acquired his first seeds. Those germinated. Not to be outdone, the little New Hampshire vixen began to produce as well. Paul was in seed heaven.

He quickly discovered that Sakurasoh are the rabbits of the plant world. As promiscuous as aquilegia, as easy with their virtue as daylilies, they mate and cross, creating an enormous diversity of strains in a range of colors from pure white through fragile pink and warm rose to neon fuchsia and a screaming cerise. The game is called selection, and Paul is a champion. Nothing escapes his eagle eye. Some strains, he concedes, are ordinary, but others, "Whew! What they pull off." As he leaps from clump to clump, he cups his hand under a cluster of shy,

BELOW: **Paul's real passion is at his feet. Beneath a richly layered background of conifers, flowering trees, and shrubs, the lavish carpet of primulas, when in full bloom, probably numbers in the millions.** RIGHT: **When Paul sees a primula he likes, he collects its seed in an effort to repeat its perform-ance. He keeps track of selections by placing the flower on a flatbed scanner and scanning it both faceup and facedown alongside its dismembered parts, show-ing the relationship between the pistil and the**

nodding heads, then points to a lacy white profile, as delicate as spun sugar, and gently touches the upturned blossom of a peppermint stripe, all the while crowing, "This is what spring is all about! I know I'm going to see new faces that I've never seen before."

Westport's Zone 6 climate is hospitable to primroses, and the Held-Sherman site is con-ducive to their culture. The soil composed of rich, partly decayed leaf duff, the filtered light from the tree canopy, the rocky crevices, the damp ground fed by stones wicking water into the soil—all feed primula pleasure. As the leaves drop from the trees overhead, the worms feast, leaving their casings behind, so Paul does not need to fertilize. "I have enough food right here in nature," he says. "If I added fertilizer, the plants would go berserk."

Come August first, the Sakurasoh literally goes underground. It becomes dormant, and the foliage disappears, preparing itself for the following spring's dramatic entrance. Paul says that is why the hot, dry summers of the Northeast do not affect it the way heat and drought kill off many a primula that does not go dormant. "The Sakurasoh is a very easy plant for us to grow," Paul says. "It does all the right things for this climate. It's a tough survivor." To fill the areas left empty when primroses sleep, Paul planted foamflower (*Tiarella cordifolia*), a

stamen; leaving the scanner lid open creates a black background for the flowers. The scans are labeled and stored on a compact disk.

semi-evergreen ground cover with fluffy white flowers; *Gentiana scabra,* with trailing blue flowers; and tall late-summer *Hibiscus moscheutos* with plate-size pink flowers.

From the beginning Paul experimented. By collecting seeds—one flower can produce up to a hundred seeds—he produced "explosions" of different forms. "A hundred seeds can make a hundred varieties," he explains. He dedicated the area behind his barn to working with new discoveries, and as he selected, he segregated, giving each form a one-foot-square territory. Soon he had a hundred squares.

LEFT: **In Japan, Sakurasoh are traditionally cultivated in pots, as collectors believe that the flower, to be appreciated, should be held at eye level. A glazed pot, essential to the aesthetics, should hold four to five plants, depending on the size of the flower. Each year the plants are divided to keep the same number of plants growing in a pot, a practice Paul uses as a model when potting his own primroses—like 'Ballet Queen', one of his selections.**

Japanese collectors set up *kadans,* **homemade Sakurasoh theaters that traditionally contain five shelves, each holding eight pots across. Although Paul is dismayed at the idea of a mere forty pots, he notes, "The Japanese have small yards; I have two acres. When they see me growing Sakurasoh in the ground, they 'ooh' and 'ahh.' I am blessed to have all this space." Of course he can't wait to build a** *kadan.*

He planted many out in the garden, where they formed colonies and produced unusual offspring, which he plucked out and brought back to his testing station. He transplanted the finest selections to pots, which now line several tables at the side of the house. The primulas' only pest seems to be the vine weevil, a starch-craving grub that climbs into the pots and devours the rhizomes. In waging his ongoing war against the nasty creatures, Paul has set the tables' sawhorse feet into containers filled with a mixture of unpleasant substances like castor oil and kerosene.

Success bred desire, and Paul wanted more. In 1988, Richard Critz, the editor of the American Primrose Society's newsletter, presented a slide show based on an article by Kazuo Hara of Japan. Paul recognized certain characteristics of named Japanese forms that seemed to have appeared in his own hybrids. After all, this primrose originated on the floodplains of Japan.

Sakurasoh history reads like an adventure story, woven with many tales, which the teacher in Paul is only too willing to recount. In Japan the Sakurasoh was a revered plant, as far back as the sixteenth century. The samurai, the warrior classes, while not wealthy, had a taste for art and beauty. They collected Sakurasoh, named more than a thousand varieties, and sold

TOP: **As a subtle complement to the colorful primulas, Paul plants masses of understated plants, like hostas, ferns, and tiarella.** RIGHT: **Images of Sakurasoh are found throughout Japanese decoration, from stonework on buildings to kimonos, manhole covers, and these stamps, a souvenir of Paul's 1996 trip to attend Sakurasoh Day celebrations and see the plant growing in its natural habitat.** OPPOSITE: **Through the exchange of rhizomes with collectors in Japan, Paul has acquired numerous Japanese named varieties.** CLOCKWISE FROM TOP LEFT: **'Izayoi', 'Hokuto Sei', 'Hakusa Seisho', 'Tamagawa', 'Yume-dono', 'Uzino Miyako', 'Masahiro Shiino', and 'Hakusa Seisho'.** CENTER: **'Miyabi no'.**

them to the shoguns, who cherished flowers. Many of those old varieties remain in circulation. In the mid–nineteenth century Philipp Franz van Siebold, a German physician and plant hunter, found the Sakurasoh in Japan and brought it back to Leiden, where he established a nursery to introduce Japanese plants to Europe. Hence the Western taxonomy *Primula sieboldii*.

Today almost every town in Japan has its own Sakurasoh society; the Tokyo organization has more than 600 members. That number exceeds the total of the American Primrose Society's world membership of 450, which includes collectors in all 30-plus sections of the genus, 600 species of the plant. In 1994 Paul started the American Sakurasoh Association, a somewhat esoteric organization that boasts 150 members worldwide. Each member receives not only a newsletter hot off Paul's computer but also 400 seeds of his precious primroses

annually. Ever generous, when Paul strikes gold, he shares the wealth. When he received a cache of rhizomes of Japanese forms from across the Pacific, he divided them among his members.

Paul's primrose path has been far from idyllic. The Japanese connection took persistence; language was a barrier. But Paul's ardor for the flower was contagious. He wrote—in English—to all ten Japanese members of the American Primrose Society. He now has a translator, the mother of one of his students, for whom he named a purple-and-white lacy-edged selection: 'Setuko'.

The Japanese generally propagate by rhizome division rather than by seed, since the plants often do not come true from seed—that unpredictable charm that so delights Paul. When he first secured seed, from Japan, it was old, and germination was spotty. These days, however, it is rhizomes that travel between Paul and Japan, and he propagates by rhizome division in his own garden as well.

Paul tracks his Sakurasoh collection on his computer. Over a hundred of his own forms now have names, many selected by his wife and children and reflecting such things as family food preferences, as in 'Blueberries and Cream' or 'Purple Plum'. 'Eye-Bright' was named for its star-shaped center, 'Waverly' for its wavy edge. Perhaps the most tender of Held's Strains, a peachy pink beauty with a soft face, is called 'My Love Jane'.

SAKURASOH FROM SEED
Planting Primulas

SAKURASOH CELEBRATE our Independence Day by setting seed. On about July 4, "just as soon as school is out," Paul Held begins his harvest. He must bag the seed before the little plants hurl their progeny out into the landscape. The process takes three full days. With the flower petals gone, only the stems and calyxes are left. He gathers all of them and drops them into paper shopping bags, "which breathe," then he carefully labels the bags with the names of the strains or forms.

Over the next weeks, the contents of the bags dry, making it easier to separate the calyx and stem from the seed. Paul stores the seed in the refrigerator in labeled glass jars. He adds a drop of water to each jar to maintain a hint of moisture.

Seed can be sown anytime between November and February. Paul cautions that plants grown out of the ground, in flats or pots, need to be covered in the winter, as frost can heave them out of their containers, killing them on the spot.

His preferred planting medium is one part sand, one part peat, and one part loam. He adds a couple of teaspoons of an evenly balanced slow-release fertilizer to approximately two bushels of the medium. Paul claims that the seeds "sense" the presence of food, and that adding a small amount of fertilizer helps to initiate germination.

'Eye Catcher', a Held strain

Paul smooths the planting medium even with the top of the flats, then compacts it with a flat wooden block to which he has attached a handle. To deter weeds, he spreads another mixture—one-half screened sand, one-fourth peat moss, and one-fourth sterile soil—one-fourth to one-half inch deep over the top, then tamps it down.

Paul shakes the pinhead-size seeds onto a piece of white paper, where they are easier to see and to control, and slides them evenly over the top of the planting medium, using approximately four hundred seeds per container. He attached a .22-caliber rifle shell to the end of a stick to form a scoop. "I counted all four hundred seeds the first time," he explains. "This shell-scoop gives me exactly that number."

To get even distribution of the seeds, Paul recommends sowing them in a crisscross pattern, dropping seeds in one direction and then in the other. He tamps the seeds securely in place, so that they do not fall into crevices in the soil. "Never cover the Sakurasoh seeds with soil," Paul cautions. "They germinate on the surface." When he puts the flat directly outdoors with no protection, Paul dusts the surface with $\frac{1}{16}$-inch of terrarium grit, a natural quartz, so that the seeds will not be disturbed by rainfall.

"If there is no rain, you must water by misting every single day. You become like a farmer milking the cows. January, February, and March go by," Paul reflects, "and, then one day in April, the sun comes out, and the plants pop like popcorn, one right after another."

Unlike mature plants, Sakurasoh infants do not contain enough starch in their rhizomes to go dormant in August, so they keep growing, developing that starch. They are fragile and must be kept moist, especially on hot summer days.

The following spring, after they have developed their first leaves, they can be thinned or pricked out and put in pots or planted in the garden. They may flower that spring. Each year Sakurasoh develop new rhizomes, the roots at the ends of the flower stems, which is how they creep along through the garden. Old rhizomes die out and become humus.

"And as you can see," Paul adds, "these plants are happy campers. I'd like to be the Johnny Appleseed of Sakurasoh, spreading their seeds from coast to coast."

WITCHES'-BROOM

Justin C. Harper
Moline, Illinois

SOME PEOPLE roam cemeteries in search of historical data. Others make rubbings of old headstones. But Justin Harper knows that while cemeteries pay tribute to past generations, they also host a great living resource—massive mature trees. One of those old trees may harbor a treasure: a witches'-broom.

Home ownership, he explains, changes over the years; highways and shopping malls are built; towns expand . . . and trees get cut down. But in old cemeteries, which in the Midwest may date as far back as the 1860s, trees have remained where they were planted. "That's where you often find the oldest and biggest trees," observes Chub, a nickname that has stuck with Justin since childhood. "And, for us, the hunt is on. We are going brooming."

Eerie growths of great beauty, witches'-brooms are true

Justin C. Clapper

"You can do a whole lot in ten years."

aberrations of nature. For a conifer aficionado like Chub, discovering one is tantamount to finding the Holy Grail, for it is from these strange mutations that many of our most choice modern conifers are bred. Appearing as dense clusters of branches, brooms usually range in size from small balls to whopping bushel baskets. They may emerge on trees as the apical, or terminal, growths or they may develop on side branches. Elusive, they are often camouflaged by the host plant or surrounding vegetation.

Chub mentions 'Blue Stop Light', a dwarf conifer propagated from a broom that he discovered on a 50-foot Colorado blue spruce (*Picea pungens*) at an intersection near his home. "I drove by that broom for years. Then one day, while waiting for the light to change, I saw it for the first time. How I could have missed it all those years is amazing."

Chub has not always been so dedicated to conifers, although he included them in his garden plans from the beginning. "I went from being interested in conifers to really flipping out over them." Yet his collecting juices have always flowed. His yard has expanded into three connected gardens. He and his wife, Anna, who with a slightly raised eyebrow says of his habit, "Thank goodness we don't both do this," bought their home on a dead-end street in Moline in 1954. They soon purchased an adjacent lot and then leased a third in 1976, giving them a total of about 1½ acres. Chub also built a greenhouse.

Meticulous maintenance, the sign of Chub's gardening style, naturally extends to his outside professional activities. Originally from Lincoln, Nebraska, he earned a degree in dairy science at the University of Nebraska under the G.I. Bill. After graduating, he moved to Moline and served as the city's milk sanitarian. His journey through horticulture began when he started a landscape design and maintenance business. To further educate himself, he and Anna have traveled around the world and have visited all fifty states. Wherever he goes, he heads straight for the botanical gardens to study plants.

In the early 1960s William A. Hewitt, chairman of John Deere & Company, hired Chub to maintain the 1,300-acre grounds of the corporation's executive headquarters. "He became my mentor," Chub recalls, and as the grounds superintendent, the landscape was under Chub's care for twenty-five years. "I was lucky," he says. "My vocation and avocation were the same. I enjoyed my job so much, it didn't make any difference to me what day of the week it was."

Now retired for more than a decade, Chub has the time to pursue his conifer passion full-time. An elder statesman of the conifer world, Chub defines his mission as "preserving genetic diversity found in witches'-brooms and other fine conifer selections." It is also important, he says, that someday people can look at plants he propagated and say, "That's what he did way back then." He adds, "They may have better plants, but my plants will give them something with which to compare the new."

Chub has given conifer lovers much to admire. Three times he has assembled an enviable

PREVIOUS PAGES, LEFT: **The 'Bingman Broom', discovered in Edginton, Illinois, in 1986, is top-grafted to a European larch (*Larix decidua*). The understock has been allowed to grow on the same plant to highlight the broom's tight growth.** RIGHT: ***Pinus sylvestris* 'Hillside Creeper', living up to its name, spreads across the end**

of a wide bed. It turns "a beautiful butter yellow" during the winter months. A yellow-to-silver variegated upright Wares arborvitae (*Thuja occidentalis* 'Warenana Lutescens') contrasts with the pine in habit and color. THIS PAGE, ABOVE: *Pinus strobus* **'Cockerton' from a witches'-broom.**

RIGHT: **In an immaculately manicured garden, a private arboretum, Chub Harper maintains a superb array of conifers. Over the years, Chub has grown more than a thousand different varieties, always refining his collection. The densely needled mounding specimen in the foreground is** *Thuja occidentalis* **'Hetz Midget'.** FAR RIGHT AND BELOW: *Sciadopitys verticillata* **'Wintergreen'; the Japanese Umbrella Pine, with its glossy needles, is reported to be one of the hardiest forms of this conifer species.**

array of conifers, many of them offspring of witches'-brooms. Twice, when his garden looked perfect, he dug up more than three hundred conifers and gave them away, setting up separate collections in two arboretums, one in Michigan and the other in Iowa.

The term "witches'-broom" comes from the German word *Hexenbesen. Hex* means to "witch" and a besom is a bundle of twigs tied together and used for sweeping. It is not surprising that these inexplicable growths that look like brooms gave rise to superstition in medieval Europe. Some believed that witches created the formations and used them as roosts. Others thought they were inhabited by elves, hobgoblins, and evil spirits. Modern-day broom hounds joke that it is no coincidence that brooms are often found in cemeteries.

A born storyteller and teacher, Chub is eager to explain his methods of propagating these rare plants. There are two kinds of witches'-brooms. Pathogenic brooms are caused by known organisms: insects, viruses, fungi, or hemiparasites like mistletoe. These "diseased brooms" indicate blight on sick plants and are useless to the collector, as they are not sources for new genetic material and cannot be propagated. "Nor would any collector want to propagate them," observes Chub.

But the second, the nonpathogenic group, is a fount of mystery and magic for conifer mavens. These witches'-brooms appear on otherwise seemingly normal plants. Not only will the density of their structure be different—usually much tighter—from the host or mother plant, but their needles may be smaller and their colors more unusual, often deeper and richer. As unique genetic mutations they offer an opportunity to produce offspring with characteristics completely different from those displayed by the host. "These brooms are the source of many of our dwarf and miniature conifers," Chub explains.

Even scientifically oriented conifer-mad specialists, like Chub, cannot explain the origin of nonpathogenic brooms, though theories abound. A hypothesis that has been tested in Colorado points to the fact that more brooms appear on the southeast sides of mountains, where plants receive more radiation from the sun, and that the increased radiation may cause the terminal bud to mutate. Location is another consideration: plants that grow in wind channels, where dust and foreign material rough up the surface of the bark of the mother tree, are more likely to sport brooms. But experts hasten to add that this is all speculation. "We don't

understand all we know," says Chub, after thirty years of exploring this still uncharted territory, and after having personally discovered over four hundred brooms.

Nature is rarely so accommodating as to place a broom in a spot where collectors can walk up and pick a sample, like a piece of fruit. Usually brooms are sky high. To retrieve their tiny, twig-sized quarry Chub and his colleague, Randy Dykstra, invented a collapsible pole pruner, made from a roof rake topped by a pruning head. Several 6-foot aluminum pole extensions allow the tool to extend to 45 feet. If the broom is still unreachable, up goes a freestanding A-frame extension ladder. And as a last resort? They shoot the broom out of the tree. Chub tells of one broom that hung way out over the Mississippi River. One of the men took aim and shot a sample off the broom; they collected it as it floated on the water's surface. Those gymnastics, he admits, are hard to explain to onlookers.

Once the prize is retrieved, it is bagged in plastic and placed in a cooler to prolong its life. If Chub has compatible understock, the grafting operation can occur immediately. Otherwise, stock must be acquired from another propagator, or the scion must be sent to the other collector for propagation.

LEFT AND ABOVE: **One of the most magnificent specimens in Chub's garden is a European larch (*Larix decidua* 'Pendula'). Now about 15 years old, its weeping form was created by a series of nine grafts in the upper branches. It takes on different personalities as the light changes throughout the day. In the foreground are *Pinus sylvestris* 'Hillside Creeper' and *Picea abies* 'Nidiformis'. Chub has had many horticultural interests, including roses, bearded irises, and daylilies. However, for the last thirty years his primary focus has been conifers. He observes, "The longer one is into horticulture, the more specialized one becomes." Chub's planting style, a layering of form and texture, alternates creeping or low-mounding conifers, like the *Pinus sylvestris* in the foreground, with upright varieties, like Wares arborvitae or the weeping larch. The effect is a complex pattern in infinite shades of green, restful and rich at the same time.**

Brooms are used as propagation material in three main ways. Rooting the cutting is a desirable technique, but one the collected specimen often resists. Pines almost never root from cuttings, probably because the resin, which carries the nutrients, hardens quickly, preventing the cutting from forming roots. However, Chub notes, when this method does work, it is more likely to maintain the characteristics of the original broom. The second technique involves the use of seed collected from the broom, although brooms rarely set viable seed.

Broad, sweeping lawns and narrow grass paths separate the conifer display beds. While a few conifers, like firs, are miserable in Moline's summer heat, and certain species of *Chamaecyparis* and *Cryptomeria* refuse to put up with the winters, a wide range flourish in Chub's Zone 5A climate. Crisply edged curvilinear beds are mulched with 3 inches of shredded hardwood bark against weeds. A dwarf Norway spruce (*Picea abies* 'Pumila'), one of Chub's recommendations, grows in a broad mound in the foreground. FAR RIGHT: The variegated needles of *Taxus × media* 'Helen Corbit', a rounded shrub-form yew, turn to green later in the season. BELOW: *Picea occidentalis* 'Holmstrup'. Chub says that conifers are low-maintenance plants. "And they look gorgeous all winter." He adds, "I've never had a hosta nut call in November and say, 'Come look at my plants.'" Chub rarely fertilizes; since he is fostering dwarfs, he does not want to accelerate growth, except at the propagation stage. In his latest philanthropic gesture, Chub donated forty-eight large specimens from this part of his garden to the Quad City Botanical Center in 2001 to be the nucleus of its new conifer collection.

The most common method, "at least for the first go-around," is grafting. Witches'-brooms are generally old wood with little food reserve—a liability called the juvenility factor, which makes grafting the only solution. The scion is attached to compatible rootstock of equal diameter, matching up the cambium layers of each. Compatible specimens are usually of the same species. "You can't graft a spruce on a pine or vice versa," Chub cautions.

The enigma lies in the fact that the characteristics of the broom on the mother plant will not always indicate how it will look after grafting. Variables include the position on the broom from which the scion wood was collected, the nature of the understock, the climate, and the soil. In other words, the whole system is unpredictable. After all that effort, only a small percentage of the new plants are superior specimens. "Some," admits Chub, "are quite ordinary. They take a ride in the chipper. But when you find something distinctive, it's worth the whole effort."

In a new plant the first thing Chub looks for is form. He determines whether it is narrow and upright, low and flat, or graceful and weeping, and if it is a fine specimen of a particular type of habit. The second consideration, in his judgment, is color. He is looking for rich, deep greens, vivid blue-greens, or bright chartreuse-yellows. Sometimes new growth can be dramatic, maintaining its color well into the season. The third factor is texture—the elegance of the formation of the needles.

Bringing one of these super dwarfs to the market using brooms to produce nursery stock is a slow, painstaking process that may take decades. It also takes funds. Chub points out that the industry is willing to invest in the introduction of a new rose, which can stimulate an initial release of 250,000 plants. The conifer collector's world is smaller, however, and more exclusive. "A first introduction of a conifer might be only 2,000 plants." As a result, many of these discoveries reside only in arboretums or in private collections.

In 1981, Chub became a benefactor. "I donated my entire collection—conifers that ranged

in size from 6 to 15 feet—to Michigan State University's Hidden Lake Gardens." The gift, each plant hand dug, filled three semitrailer trucks and ultimately became the nucleus of the Harper Collection of Dwarf and Rare Conifers. Chub continues his involvement with the Harper Collection, frequently making the eight-hour drive to advise on design, plant editing, and other ministrations. One important consideration of such a donation, Chub says, is to work to establish an endowment for the maintenance of the collection; that effort is one of his current projects.

In 1991, having established a relationship with Frances and Robert Bickelhaupt, who had started the Bickelhaupt Arboretum on the 14 acres surrounding their home in Clinton, Iowa, Chub donated a second garden of conifers. They, too, traveled by truck to the newly named Heartland Collection of Dwarf and Rare Conifers. The collection contains mostly plants that have originated from witches'-brooms and in a few cases the original tree, complete with its broom, has been moved into the arboretum as an object lesson. Today Chub serves on the arboretum's board as vice president of operations, and since the arboretum is only forty-five minutes from his Moline home, he spends a great deal of time there, refining the collection.

"Plant people are eternal optimists. We're planting trees for the future," Chub says with a smile. "Everyone should leave this world a little better than he found it—or at least try to."

PRIME CHOICE

Justin Harper's Twenty Favorite Conifers in Four Sizes Plus His Bonus Five

CONIFERS ARE among the oldest known woody plants; more than five hundred species grow worldwide. Justin Harper says the word "conifer" comes from the Latin meaning "cone-bearing." Most of these plants produce their seed in the cones, but some conifers, like junipers and yews, make berry-like fruit. Most conifers are evergreen; however, larch and cypress and a few others drop their leaves in autumn.

While Chub's garden is groomed to perfection with nary a needle out of place, he claims conifer collecting is easy-care gardening. "These plants need little nipping and tucking; they don't require spraying," he says. Chub rarely fertilizes, emphasizing that if he is fostering dwarfs, he would choose to accelerate growth, except at the propagation stage.

Among the conifers are some of the smallest and largest living woody plants. Of special interest to gardeners are the dwarf conifers, although "dwarf" is an inexact term, even among conifer connoisseurs. As a relative guide, the American Conifer Society, of which Chub is a past president, has adopted the following four size categories for conifers.

CATEGORY	GROWTH PER YEAR	SIZE AT 10–15 YEARS
Miniature	Under 3 inches	2-3 feet
Dwarf	3-6 inches	3-6 feet
Intermediate	6-12 inches	6-15 feet
Large	12 inches and over	15 feet or more

BOTANICAL NAME	COMMON NAME
MINIATURE CONIFERS	
Picea abies 'Pumila'	Dwarf Norway spruce
Picea glauca 'Pixie'	Dwarf pixie white spruce
Pinus strobus 'Sea Urchin'	Dwarf white pine
Pseudotsuga menziesii 'Little Jon'	Dwarf Douglas fir
Tsuga canadensis 'Lewis'	Dwarf Canadian hemlock
DWARF CONIFERS	
Abies lasiocarpa 'Green Globe'	Dwarf Rocky Mountain fir
Abies koreana 'Prostrata'	Dwarf Korean fir
Picea abies 'Nidiformis'	Bird's nest Norway spruce
Picea omorika 'Nana'	Dwarf Serbian spruce
Picea pungens 'Montgomery'	Montgomery Colorado spruce
INTERMEDIATE CONIFERS	
Chamaecyparis pisifera 'Filifera Aurea'	Yellow thread leaf false cypress
Larix decidua 'Pendula'	Weeping European larch
Pinus cembra	Swiss stone pine
Pinus parviflora 'Bergman'	Bergman's Japanese white pine
Pinus sylvestris 'Hillside Creeper'	Hillside creeper Scot's pine
LARGE CONIFERS	
Chamaecyparis nootkatensis 'Pendula'	Weeping Nootka cypress
Picea omorika 'Pendula'	Weeping Serbian spruce
Pinus flexilis 'Vanderwolf's Pyramid'	Vanderwolf's limber pine
Pinus koraiensis 'Glauca'	Blue Korean pine
Taxodium distichum	Bald or swamp cypress
FIVE OF CHUB'S PERSONAL FAVORITES	
Chamaecyparis nootkatensis 'Green Arrow'	Green arrow Nootka cypress
Picea glauca 'Pendula'	Weeping white spruce
Pinus bungeana	Lacebark pine
Pinus mugo 'Mops'	Dwarf Swiss mountain pine
Thuja occidentalis 'Smaragd'	Emerald green arborvitae

CLOCKWISE FROM UPPER LEFT: *Picea abies* 'Pumila' (*Picea abies* 'Pendula' in background); *Pseudotsuga menziesii* 'Little Jon'; *Picea abies* 'Nudiformis'; *Thuja occidentalis* 'Smaragd', which Chub cautions should be trained to a central leader; *Larix decidua* 'Pendula'; *Pinus koraiensis* 'Glauca'.

SHOEHORN GARDENING

Sonny Garcia and Tom Valva
San Francisco, California

"PLANTING IN THE ground is limiting," decrees Sonny Garcia, who in partnership with Tom Valva has wedged an astonishing array of plants—more than two thousand—into a modest backyard measuring just 30 by 60 feet. Using a brilliant palette accomplished primarily with foliage color—purple, red, chartreuse, variegated, spotted, and striped—and pots mounted at varying levels, the men have created an abstract collage that is arresting and totally contemporary.

Size constraints have never stopped these gardeners, or even slowed them down. If there is no more room to move horizontally, they go up, over the top, around corners, or in any other direction where they can find open space. This is vertical gardening, many-layered, overlapping, and intertwined, at its most ingenious. Yet, far

Sonny Garcia

"Use your imagination. Anything goes."

Tom Valva

from being claustrophobic, the garden is warmly seductive. "Flowers are great," Sonny says, "a bonus, really, but to achieve year-round color a plant's foliage is its most important feature. Of course, there *are* flowers. Thirty different abutilons, twenty different fuchsias, a 6-foot-tall callalily with speckled leaves called 'White Giant', exotics like *Epacris longifolia* 'A Chorus Line', and dozens of vines, most of which produce bloom.

Gardening comes naturally to both Sonny and Tom, although this shoehorn style is strictly their own invention. Sonny remembers his mother's love of gardening and how, when he was growing up in the Philippines, he helped her arrange plants in bloom throughout the home. Tom earned his spending money as a youth caring for people's yards, often those of his teachers. When the men first met, they lived in a condo and transformed the surrounds of the mundane communal swimming pool with plant-filled pots. There they began to realize in their benign Zone 9 to 10 climate what could be achieved without ever putting a plant in the ground.

In 1985, Sonny, an architect who specializes in engineering glass and aluminum structures, and Tom, the computer manager of an insurance company, bought their home in the quiet neighborhood of Sunnyside in San Francisco. They wanted a Victorian house, but a soaring real estate market forced them to settle for a two-bedroom Mediterranean-style house, and they set out to transform it indoors and out. "We learned by doing," recalls Sonny. "He's the designer and I'm the brawn," adds Tom.

The backyard, while fenced and private, was a flat rectangle of grass with concrete walks. "Didn't appeal to me," comments Sonny. Out came all but a 4-by-8-foot patch of grass. In its place the men designed an intricate warren of paths that twist around to meet one another. "They allow a walk through the garden with sequential revelations," Sonny says. "No matter how small a garden is, you should not be able to see all of it at once."

The men decided to vary the levels of the garden, thus creating the illusion of more space. "Contrary to popular belief," says Sonny, "introducing different levels into a small garden actually makes it feel bigger." The levels, whether for person or plant, vary from a single step to a deck that towers a full story above the garden. A balcony at the opposite end of the garden is raised six steps above the main garden and topped with a pergola, a sheltered place in which to enjoy breakfast with the birds, wild or tame—including five pet parrots.

One of the most inventive methods of varying levels is the use of pots. "About a third of our plants live in pots," reflects Tom. Neither knows the precise number of pots employed, but it is certainly in excess of two hundred. Shrubs and trees as well as perennials and annuals thrive in them. The use of pots allows for changes in plant arrangements, by hoisting and

PREVIOUS PAGES, LEFT: **Stone and marble balls are a recurring theme in Sonny Garcia and Tom Valva's garden. The men's creative use of pots and pediments allows for a unique vision of vertical gardening.** TOP: **The ornaments that most delight Sonny and Tom are those that catch them by surprise. The purple pitcher was found in Mexico amongst a beach vendor's wares. The wire chair is host to the vine *Dicentra scandens*.** THIS PAGE, ABOVE: **A raised balcony at the far end of the garden offers a shaded sanctuary and a view back toward the house.**

TOP LEFT: *Tropaeolum pere-grinum,* **the canary creeper vine, has fringed flowers like a bird's wings.** TOP RIGHT: **Blue bottles hang in an iron** *tuteur.* ABOVE: **Narrow-necked pots are arranged in graduated groupings.** OPPO-SITE: **A black cast-iron bird from Japan perches on a concrete ball artfully draped with oxidized copper ivy.**

carrying—not so easy if a filled 3-foot pot weighs 60 pounds. The two men buy pots constantly, "especially Asian pots with beautiful glazes in blue, green, eggplant, and gold." The pots are arranged on an elaborate system of shelves and pedestals.

"A garden is not sustained by plants alone," says Sonny, a curious statement from the consummate plantsman. But he believes that relief from looking at plants makes for a more pleasant experience in a garden. He adds, "Sculptural or architectural ornaments, well distributed around a garden, keep the viewer's interest. These things, sometimes a little bit crazy, delight, and we aim to delight."

"At the end of every path is a focal point, a bench, an urn, or a more unconventional object," Tom adds, "and they grab your eye. They compel you toward them, and they make you ask yourself questions."

The garden is scrupulously maintained. "We're both into tidying things up," says Tom. Vigilant pruning is the key to such order—and to each arrangement. In a garden this size plants could quickly get out of hand. Here Sonny is clearly the boss. "Things that do too well, and things that don't do well, come out," he says. "Every season—every day—is a process of elimination. I like a garden that is not static, is always changing. I want to try new plants, new ideas. We even managed a gunnera (*G. manicata*), a gorgeous plant, here for a while. We allowed it three leaves. When it insisted on producing more, its time was over."

Water, from the beginning, was another challenge. For the first seven years rationing was in force in their area. They hand-watered, often using the rinse water from the washing machine. Finally, they installed an irrigation system, which reaches every plant in the ground and every pot. A network of about 100 feet of one-inch pipes leads to all areas of the garden. Quarter-inch drip pipes are teed off the main lines, twisting like bonsai wire, so Sonny can direct the

HOW TO MAKE A SMALL GARDEN SEEM BIG

Twelve Tips

Sonny and Tom create layered vignettes of plants, multihued tapestries of foliage, texture, and color. Here the arrangement includes: *Loropetalum chinense* 'Plum Delight', *Acer palmatum* 'Shaina', *Aeonium arboreum* 'Zwartkop', *Eucomis* 'Sparkling Burgundy', *Oxalis tetraphylla* 'Iron Cross', and *Geranium* 'Ann Folkard'.

1. No matter how small your garden is, it should not be seen all at once. Entice people to go around corners to see the next point of interest.

2. Camouflage the property line with a fence or foliage plants. The effect will enlarge the horizon so you do not see where the garden ends. Your boundary line will be extended.

3. Bring water into the garden. The trickle of a small fountain will shut out other noise and create a tranquil atmosphere. The sound of water is soothing to the soul.

4. Work vertically. Force the eye to look up, rather than down or straight ahead. Arrange your plants in tiers. Use vines; don't be afraid to prune their lower branches heavily if they grow too thick. Use plants in pots and place them on pedestals of varying heights. By going up, you can extend the garden measurably.

5. Keep your paths narrow. They make the perspective appear longer.

6. Make gradual changes in elevation. Go up a little at a time. Then break that rule and raise a deck several steps for a dramatic change in elevation.

7. Make the garden appear to have separate rooms. Give each one a focal point, like a pot or an ornament.

8. Use some big accent plants. It's the same principle as in interior design: you wouldn't put a lot of small furniture in a small room; that would make the room look even smaller. A big piece of furniture will give the room dramatic presence. A big plant will do the same for your garden.

9. Place mirrors strategically to reflect light in shady areas and fool the eye into thinking there is another garden beyond.

10. Use variegated and colored foliage to pull the eye forward or back. Gold or variegated foliage brightens up areas on foggy days and seems to come forward. Light grasses, gold or variegated, planted along a path can lighten up the ground. Burgundy foliage recedes and it makes a border seem deeper.

11. Move plants often. Change freshens up a garden. If plants are moved frequently, the garden will seem like a different place each time you see it.

12. Leave some portion of the garden open, even if it is not very large. An open area allows breathing room.

water very precisely. He calculates the amount of water needed and makes the appropriate number of emitter holes. Even within a single pot, one plant may receive more water than another. Scores of mini-spray heads, attached to the tops of green stakes, are also located strategically throughout the garden. On four separate zones, the system runs in the middle of every other night, twenty minutes for each zone, using only 75 to 100 gallons of water.

Feeding plants, especially those in pots, is ongoing. "I have a choice," Sonny says. "I either inject fertilizer into the automatic watering system or selectively feed; the latter is the method I prefer." He uses both a slow-release 14-14-14 and liquid fertilizers. "There is no rule of thumb. You just have to keep with the pulse of the plant." He amends the soil with well-rotted steer manure, preferring cow manure when it's available. "And turkey manure is just wonderful, if you can get it." For potted plants, he adds polymers, which often come in high-quality potting soil, to help to maintain moisture in the pots.

All these elements together—the jungle-like density of the plants, the changes of level, narrow paths, sophisticated plantsmanship, and painstaking maintenance—do not necessarily add up to enchantment. It is the men's imagination and vision that has allowed them to create magic in a molecule.

The final touch to many of Tom and Sonny's arrangements is a brilliant accent, often in the form of an exotic flowering plant. TOP LEFT: *Epacris longiflora* 'Chorus Line', an Australian native; TOP RIGHT: The northwest African *Gladiolus communis* subsp. *byzantinus*; ABOVE: The steel blue and purple bracts of the Mediterranean *Cerinthe major purpurescens*. LEFT: The bold foliage of a *Cordyline australis* 'Albertii' or a windmill palm, *Trachycarpus fortunei*, make strong statements from above.

A MULTICULTURAL MARRIAGE

Mary A. Homans
Islesboro, Maine

MARY HOMANS has lived at the edge of both the Atlantic Ocean and the Pacific. She has maintained an apartment in London and traveled all over the world. When she decided to make a new garden on Islesboro, a "rockbound" island off the coast of Maine, she determined to combine the best of her present and her past. From the experiences of her international adventures she stirred California and Maine, Europe and the Far East, woodland and rockery, native and exotic. The result: an American melting pot of gardens created by the hand of a resolute Yankee.

As a child, Mary had summered in one of the sprawling "cottages" built on Islesboro in the early twentieth century. The island, 12 miles long and 4 miles wide, has an irregular coastline; its harbors and inlets, while wild, even hostile, in a nor'easter, are ideal for

Mary A. Homans

"The more knowledge about plants that I gain, the more I realize how little I know."

warm-weather pursuits. Steeped in maritime history dating back to the seventeenth century, the island has also been a secluded playground for the well-to-do.

The Down East–style house that Mary's parents purchased in the 1930s was classic but understated, as in Maine, not Newport. It had seventeen bathrooms, a tennis court, a swimming pool, and a playhouse, as well as elaborate gardens. "During the winter in New York, my mother took every horticulture course that Columbia offered," Mary recalls. Her powerful influence gave Mary her first taste of the satisfactions of gardening. Mary and all four of her siblings had their own gardens at the island compound, where they "grew carrots and cucumbers and sold them to the cook."

Growing up surrounded by boxwood parterres, yew hedges, fountains, and rose rondels, both at home and abroad, Mary's gardening style could have followed the formal path. Her father, the late Winthrop W. Aldrich, was, after all, an international banker and the ambassador to the Court of St. James's, and with her mother's gardening interest, Mary gained entrée to many of the great English gardens. As a young married woman, Mary and her husband, a lawyer, moved to California's Bay Area, where they lived and gardened for thirty years, until her husband's death in 1969.

In 1972 Mary's father offered to build Mary a house on family land in Islesboro, and, she says, " I did not refuse." She surprised the community by building a one-story California-style redwood house with a central great room and floor-to-ceiling windows, the better to view the water. While the house—located at the southern end of the island, where winter residents number four—was built for Mary's summer use, she has made it her full-time residence since 1988.

Mary brought in Thomas D. Church, the Bay Area's innovative landscape architect, to design the grounds immediately around the new house. "Tommy," as Mary calls her friend, fostered the idea expressed in his seminal book, *Gardens Are for People,* that gardens should be outdoor living rooms with plain wooden furniture. Emphasis should be on the garden's social importance rather than its horticulture. Plants are nice, he maintained, but people are better.

"We had a fine time," Mary says. "I shot the lines for Tommy, so if something isn't straight, it's my fault." Sinuous lines being one of Thomas Church's trademarks, the entrance courtyard is a circle surrounded with raised beds in undulating shapes.

Twenty years ago Mary and her daughter, Lucy, climbed the hillside behind the house and began to imagine a new garden—a Hillside Garden. "We loved to walk, and the only place to walk back then was Route 1, so we decided to make a garden with paths for walking." She

PREVIOUS PAGES: **Between Mary Homans's house and the sea, a 500-foot lawn terminates in a spectacular display of lupins. Rugosa roses, a trademark of the seaside garden, make the border fragrant, dense, and lush.** THIS PAGE, OPPOSITE: **In a magnificent woodland and rock garden, Mary integrates her collection of northeast**

native plants with those she has gathered from around the world. ABOVE. **Two sets of oversized sliding glass doors allow a view through Mary's house across terraces to the sea beyond. A 2-foot retaining wall encloses a raised garden, featuring clusters of native birches underplanted with rhododendrons.**

gestures, sweeping her arm to indicate the scale of the 2-acre garden. "Now I have a bear by the tail. This is *not* a low-maintenance garden."

Mary invited Karl Grieshaber, the now-retired curator of the Native Plant Garden at New York Botanical Garden, to help lay out the paths. She recalls, "We had two chain saw operators, a front-end loader, and a backhoe. We took out 250 trash trees, little spruces that were too crowded. We left the native birches and some tall spruces, balsams, ashes, and maples."

ABOVE: **One of the most stunning features of Mary's woodland hillside is the rich carpet into which she has woven masses of plants in rhythmic patterns, echoing the waves of the sea. The shades of green seem infinite, as ferns, hostas, gingers, sweet woodruff, and lady's mantle overlap in exquisite textural patterns. "Whenever I make a new garden, I divide hostas, and I already have a start."**

To Mary's delight the heavy equipment revealed rock ledges, which she washed using a hose and a broom. Stumps were pulled out as high up the hill as the backhoe was able to maneuver; the rest were left to decay. Shapely boulders, deposited by glaciers, were coaxed to different locations as dramatic accents. "Karl laid out the paths, and even recommended initial plants, like the mugo pines."

After that Mary was on her own. "We did everything ourselves," she recalls. "We filled the pockets in the rock with soil, adding gritty peastone and compost, compost, compost." She began to collect plants from all over the world. "It's one thing to have plants, rare or not, it's another to make their placement with each other aesthetically beautiful. I consider texture, contrast, color, and scale, but I don't always take my own wise advice."

Because a portion of the hillside is open to the sky, protected and sunny, it became a rock garden. Paths were finished in three-quarter-inch gravel, which is also used as mulch around a collection of alpine plants, like saxifrages, *Dryas octopetala,* and late-flowering gentians. Some, like *Ramonda myconi,* with its purple flowers and crinkled leaves, prefer more shade;

they live farther up the hill. "I bought a rosette of ramonda in 1980. She finally died, but she left her self-sown children in the crevices," Mary observes.

The area farther up the hill, in the shade of the tall firs, became a woodland, with paths cushioned in pine needles and edged with the cut trunks of birch trees, elements in keeping with the natural feeling of the garden. Flowering understory trees—dogwoods, amelanchiers magnolias, and redbuds—were all planted generously. Rhododendrons, which

BELOW: **"It took five years for moss to blanket the rocks,"** Mary recalls. To hasten the action on the stumps, she moved pads of moss from the woods and patted them

into place. LEFT: At its highest point, the garden is punctuated by a rustic toolshed, which Mary bought at a flower show in Bangor: "Now if I forget something, I don't have to go all the way down the hill," she explains. She may forget a tool, but she never forgets a plant. How does she keep track of so many? "By memory."

MARVELS IN MINIATURE
Trough Gardens

MARY HOMANS'S Hillside Garden is a microcosm of the contrasts that characterize her property. On one hand, it is a woodland and rockery on a grand scale. However, she also has made a reputation for just the opposite—worlds in miniature.

Lining the wall outside her house and filling the shelves of a plant stand is a series of trough gardens,

creatively designed and meticulously maintained. Mary says that "each one is supposed to look like a piece of the woodland. People walk up to them, for their small scale acts like a magnet."

Many of the dwarf plants that Mary favors—andromeda, cassiope, enkianthus, gaultheria, kalmia, pieris, rhododendron, azalea, vaccinium—are commonly grown full-scale in gardens. "People do not realize that the families of so many of these plants have dwarf members."

Most of Mary's troughs are made of traditional cast stone or cement. A few, which are as old as the house, were made by the carpenters out of the original red-wood. Ceramic containers with interesting exterior glaze, color, or shape also attract her. Mary makes sure that each container has two or three holes in the bottom, for good drainage is essential.

She wants the planting medium to be "not quite stony and very free draining." For a trough she chooses plants that like the same soil conditions; many of her selec-

tions are ericaceous. Her rule-of-thumb mixture, which may be varied because of the particular demands of a group of plants, is "one-third gravel, one-third compost, one-third leaf mold, plus a little lime if you have a lime-lover."

The same aesthetic principles apply to trough gardening as to creating a full-scale garden, she says. Think texture, contrast, color, scale—"some tall, some small, and some in between, with a concentration on foliage that is tiny." Because the whole garden occupies such a small space, the design is less forgiving.

In spite of being labeled as dwarfs, these plants can outgrow their little homes. "When they get too big for the troughs, I move them out into the garden. Troughs are not planted for life."

thrive in the slightly acidic soil, were planted in clusters. A favorite is *R. schlippenbachii,* commonly—and aptly—called the royal azalea. It has huge, pale pink flowers in the spring, and Mary describes its fall color as "like the inside of a cantaloupe." She calls attention to *R. yakusimanum*, a tight mound with a thick reddish brown indumentum, like velvet, on the new foliage. *R. bureavii,* too, features a gray indumentum turning to copper.

Mary also encouraged native ferns, which she augmented with others, like *Adiantum venustum,* the diminutive black-stemmed Himalayan maidenhair fern. "Ferns do a lot in a garden," Mary says. "Their grace covers up a lot of sins." Feeling that "moss gives a woodland atmosphere and feeling of permanence," Mary has encouraged it to spread across rocks and stumps.

An open bowl at the bottom of the hill remains grassy, a visual counterpoint to the densely planted hillside. On one side is a circular garden raised with a wall, where plants like *Lewisia cotyledon* enjoy good drainage. Mary felt that the lower part of the garden "needed some weight in the design to balance the hillside," so a hundred feet of old stone wall was brought from the mainland "over there in America."

The clearing contains island beds featuring stately conifers. At its edge sits a 10-by-10-foot pond constructed on the site of an old open well. "It is fed by five springs, so the water is pretty clear, but my little pond is totally fake, made of fabric liner," Mary admits. Shrubs include a compact pink-flowered, fragrant *Daphne retusa.* An *Ulmus parvifolia* with white-edged foliage also stands at the shady edge. In the spring "it starts very pale and then slowly turns green, looking like a ghost," says Mary. Because of her garden's scale, Mary's habit is to plant in multiples; that pattern holds even by the small pond. "Three to five plants are good; a swath is better," she believes.

"I hate to admit that we have done some things backwards," Mary says. "We installed the watering system after we did the planting." There are eight outlets in the garden. "And I do throw some food around, but not so much that the plants get bigger than they are supposed to." Since Mary's soil is neutral leaning to acid, many of the plants she chooses are ericaceous—that is, they belong to the family *Ericaceae* and require soil with a pH of 6.5 or less. "Plants are pretty adaptable," she adds. "Trilliums take some lime, but I can grow them."

Mary studies plants' natural habitats or visits them, often traveling with like-minded plantaholics—in the Rockies and the Blue Ridge Mountains; in Vancouver, England, Scotland, and the Dolomites in Italy; on both the French and the Spanish sides of the Pyrenees in the Swiss Alps; and in Greece, New Zealand, Japan, and China. A license from the Department of Agriculture allows her to bring plants into this country. "You have to bring the plant in bare root. You wash all soil off the roots, then wrap a little damp facial tissue around the roots. Not all plants will take that treatment." However, she says, "I don't see the point of growing something that really doesn't like it here—unless, of course, it is a very rare plant. . . ." Her voice drifts off, perhaps as she savors her delight in finally landing a *Glaucidium palmatum.*

Mary reviews her work from the last two decades and respects the ongoing intervention by nature, the native plants that have come unannounced or by invitation. "God has been my best partner. Often plants arrive and arrange themselves in much better configurations than I could ever conceive myself."

"Whenever I plant, I think of a plant's native habitat and try to duplicate those conditions," Mary notes. A protected clearing at the lower part of the hill is hospitable to her collection of alpine plants, like saxifrages, lewisias, and late-flowering gentians. To guard the plants from the island's ravenous deer population, the entire garden is enclosed with an electric fence.

WEAVING A WOODLAND CARPET
Mary Homans's Perennial Plant List

PLANT NAME	HEIGHT	DESCRIPTION
Alchemilla alpina alpine lady's-mantle	8 inches	Deeply lobed leaves, deep green and smooth above, silver and hairy underneath; loose cymes of tiny yellow-green flowers
Alchemilla erythropoda	8–12 inches	Sharp-toothed, hairy, bluish green leaves; cymes of yellowish green flowers
Arisaema sikokianum	12–20 inches	Two pedate leaves, one 3-lobed and one 5-lobed, sometimes variegated with silver; bears large, purple-brown spathe revealing white spadix
Arisaema triphyllum jack-in-the-pulpit	6–24 inches	Leaves divided into three narrow oblong-to-ovate leaflets; bears hooded green, often dark purple–striped spathes, followed by red berries in autumn
Aruncus aethusifolius	10 inches	Pinnate, deeply cut leaves; panicles of creamy white flowers
Asarum canadense	8 inches	Heart-shaped leaves; small, brownish purple flowers
Asarum europaeum	8 inches	Rounded, glossy dark green leaves; small greenish purple flowers
Aster macrophyllus	9 inches	Dark green heart-shaped leaves; branching pale lilac daisy-like flowers
Chyrsogonum virginianum	10 inches	Heart-shaped to ovate-oblong leaves; star-shaped yellow flowers
Clintonia borealis bluebead lily	12 inches	Lance-shaped to ovate glossy, pale green leaves; loose umbels of nodding, bell-shaped greenish yellow flowers
Clintonia umbellulata	15 inches	Oblong leaves a foot long; white flowers spotted with green and purple
Epimedium × rubrum	12 inches	2½–4-inch-long pointed leaves, flushed red when young, turning red and reddish brown in autumn, crimson and pale yellow flowers

Alchemilla alpina

Epimedium × rubrum

Aruncus aethusifolius

Galium odoratum sweet woodruff	12 inches	Lance-shaped to elliptic emerald-green leaves; star-shaped scented white flowers in late spring
Gentiana acaulis trumpet gentian	4 inches	Lance-shaped, dark green leaves; deep blue, trumpet-shaped flowers
Gentiana asclepiadea willow gentian	24 inches	Willow-like, lance-shaped midgreen leaves; trumpet-shaped dark blue to light blue flowers
Geranium macrorrhizum scented cranesbill	20 inches	Seven-lobed, sticky, aromatic light green leaves; umbel-like clusters of pink to purplish pink flowers
Geranium maculatum spotted geranium	24 inches	Five- to seven-lobed glossy, midgreen leaves; upward-facing lilac-pink to bright pink flowers
Geranium sanguineum var. *striatum* (was *G. lancastrense*)	6 inches	Long, deeply cut leaves; pale pink flowers, veined darker red

Helleborus niger 'Potter's Wheel'	12 inches	Leathery, dark green leaves; large bowl-shaped flowers with green eyes
Hepatica nobilis	4 inches	Rounded or kidney-shaped midgreen leaves; silky, hairy, and purple-tinted beneath; bowl-shaped white, pink, or blue flowers
Hosta × 'June'	14–16 inches	Gold leaves, marked and edged with gray-blue; lavender flowers
Hosta Lancifolia, var. *albomarginata*	12 inches	Lance-shaped, thin, glossy green leaves, edged in white funnel-shaped purple flowers
Jeffersonia diphylla (twinleaf)	8 inches	Kidney-shaped, deeply cleft leaves; solitary cup-shaped white flowers
Jeffersonia dubia	8 inches	Kidney-shaped or rounded, two-lobed blue-green leaves; solitary cup-shaped blue or white flowers
Maianthemum canadense	8 inches	Ovate, almost stalkless midgreen leaves; racemes of fragrant white flowers followed by pale red berries
Polygonatum biflorum Solomon's seal	32 inches	Arching stems bearing alternate, narrow lance-shaped leaves; pendent greenish white flowers
Polygonatum humile	8 inches	Lance-shaped to ovate leaves on upright stems; pendent, tubular white flowers
Primula kisoana	8 inches	Rounded, shallow-lobed midgreen leaves; umbels of tubular to funnel-shaped rose to white flowers
Pulmonaria angustifolia	10 inches	Lance-shaped, unspotted mid- to dark green leaves; funnel-shaped, rich blue flowers
Pulmonaria 'Excalibur'	10 inches	Shiny, silvery white ovate leaves with deep green midribs and narrow, deep green margins; funnel-shaped violet-blue flowers
Pulmonaria officinalis 'Sissinghurst White'	12 inches	8–10-inch-long leaves with numerous white spots; pure white flowers, opening from pink buds
Ramonda myconi	4 inches	Broadly ovate, slightly crinkled leaves; flat five-petaled violet flowers

Aster macrophyllus

Pulmonaria officinalis 'Sissinghurst White'

Asarum europaeum

Ranunculus ficaria 'Brazen Hussy'	2 inches	Glossy, deep chocolate brown leaves; shining golden yellow flowers with a bronze reverse
Sedum kamtschaticum	4 inches	Lance-shaped to spoon-shaped glossy deep green leaves; star-shaped deep golden yellow flowers
Shortia galacifolia Oconee bells	6 inches	Rounded, blunt-toothed, glossy dark green leaves with wavy margins, turning bronze in fall; solitary funnel-shaped white flowers
Shortia soldanelloides var. *ilicifolia*	4–12 inches	Ovate to rounded coarse-toothed dark green leaves; trumpet-shaped white or pink flowers
Tricyrtis hirta	32 inches	Lance-shaped, veined, hairy pale green leaves; funnel-shaped purple-spotted white flowers
Tricyrtis latifolia	32 inches	Ovate-oblong, veined, glossy leaves; upward-facing white flowers
Trillium cernuum (nodding trillium)	16 inches	Diamond-shaped, abruptly pointed midgreen leaves; pale pink, reddish brown, or white flowers with wavy recurved petals

SANCTUARY

Margaret Kerr
The Springs, East Hampton, Long Island, New York

EARLY IN THE summer of 1986 Margaret Kerr got down on her hands and knees, a pile of bricks at her side. As she picked one up, then another, the pattern for her new garden's floor began to take shape. That moment was a turning point. "I never dreamed that making a garden would change my life so dramatically," recalls Marggy, as she is called. An artist who had previously worked with traditional materials—ink, paint, and mixed media—on paper and canvas, she had discovered a new medium.

The garden courtyard she built that summer was done in a simple herringbone pattern, but it was the genesis of a bold idea. By the end of August, Marggy was so comfortable handling bricks that she decided to move to the other side of the house and create two brick rugs in the landscape. For these, rather than customary

Margaret Kerr

"Middle Eastern tribal geometric carpets had become part of my subconscious over many, many years."

bricklayer's patterns, she turned to the tribal rugs on her living room floor for inspiration.

Influences and interests from her past came together and clicked over those few intense months of 1986, and Marggy embarked on a new body of work, marrying ancient traditions to a modern innovation. In fifteen years Marggy has created nine brick carpets in her own garden, as well as numerous commissions for clients' gardens and sculptural pieces using brick and the ghost images produced by manipulating brick dust on heavy rag paper that she has exhibited in galleries around the country.

"I had always admired the warmth and subtle color variation of old brick and the feeling that its manufacture and use reach back through ten thousand years of history," Marggy recalls, "but I had never used it in my work. However, when we moved to this house, I knew exactly what kind of garden I wanted—a patterned courtyard of brick, featuring medieval herbs. That was the first step." A powerful influence on Marggy's fondness for patterning, she now realizes, was her parents' collection of antique Oriental and Islamic carpets. As an adult, following their lead, she had acquired several "very worn" rugs.

Marggy had also been studying medieval gardens; as with the rugs, she was attracted to the order and symmetry of their geometric plans. She also relished the plants' names: naked

PREVIOUS PAGES, TOP LEFT, TOP RIGHT: **In Margaret Kerr's garden, a pergola covered with climbing roses (*R.* 'New Dawn') and fall-blooming clematis leads to the enclosed herb garden.** BOTTOM LEFT: **Marggy installed one of her brick carpets, titled "Peace Offering," in a secluded glade below her studio.** THIS PAGE, ABOVE: **An 8-foot-square, 4-foot-deep lily pond sits flush with the brick floor of the garden. "Medieval gardens customarily featured water at their centers," Marggy notes.** LEFT: **The meadows around the complex of buildings are left unmown throughout the season, allowing the daffodils to ripen and the native wildflowers to go to seed.**

TOP: Directly influenced by tribal carpets on her living room floor, the Rug Garden, Marggy's second series of brick carpets in the landscape, is located on the opposite side of the house from the herb garden. ABOVE: Favoring single-flowering daffodils, Marggy plants forty to fifty bulbs in a group, about one-third each of early, mid-season, and late-blooming.

ladies or *les dames sans chemises* (*Colchicum autumnale*), cuckoopint (*Arum maculatum*), St.-Mary's-thistle (*Silybum marianum*), Our-Lady's-blanket (*Stachys byzantina*), love-in-a-mist (*Nigella damascena*), and herb of grace (*Ruta graveolens*). All were cultivated in monastery gardens, and each plant had a use, whether culinary, medicinal, or aromatic. Remembering a trip to the Cloisters in New York when she was a teenager, Marggy returned years later to the museum to study its gardens, particularly the Bonnefont Cloister garden. She bought a slim volume called *Sweet Herbs and Sundry Flowers* by Tania Bayard, and it became her bible. She studied the Unicorn Tapestries woven in the fifteenth century, and was particularly smitten by the millefleur carpets of ground cover through which "a thousand flowers" grew. But it took a new home—a huge blank canvas, or landscape—for Marggy to make her first ingenious carpets—both in brick and in plants.

Marggy and her husband, abstract expressionist painter Robert Richenburg, moved to the Springs on Long Island from Ithaca, New York, in 1983 after renting houses nearby for three summers. The couple purchased a silvered-shingle house on two acres overlooking the Acabonack Harbor.

They kept the natural feeling of the land, which sweeps from the house site to wetlands and the harbor. "I didn't want to contradict the landscape," Marggy recalls. The buildings and gardens, a cozy enclave, are surrounded with drifts of daffodils—now 15,000 in number—and long grasses. To allow the native grasses to set seed these areas are never mowed until Thanksgiving. In April the scene suggests a medieval poet's "flowery mead." Close to the house, where their diminutive stature can be appreciated, Marggy favors miniature daffodils: the bulbocodium, triandrus, and cyclamineus.

The gardens snuggle close to the house, as they might have done in the Middle Ages. "I concentrated my urge for patterns in the courtyard and the beds and borders around the house," Marggy says. "I like the notion of a formal structure filled with exuberant plantings." The main 26-by-48-foot garden is contained, like a historic *hortus conclusus,* by buildings and a swimming pool on three sides and by a fence and pergola on the fourth. In a walled or cloistered garden, Marggy observes, "there is a concentrated essence, like a wonderful perfume. Fragrance is intensified, as are all the experiences of the garden. Something deep within us responds to a small, enclosed garden." In the garden's center, as its focus, is a lily pond—a family tradition.

Living in Ithaca, where they both attended Cornell University, Marggy and her first husband, William Kerr, a lawyer, had raised three children: Blake, Garry, and Meg. Marggy was only forty in 1973, when Bill tragically passed away. Throughout their marriage Marggy and Bill had a clear demarcation of indoor-outdoor duties: Marggy cared for the inside of their home and Bill maintained the yard. When Bill died, the outdoors fell to Marggy as well, and she threw herself into it wholeheartedly. "I began to garden in earnest, always with my children's encouragement and help," she says. "I studied garden design down through history, but from the start I was drawn to the medieval period. And I did a great deal of thinking about how to approach gardening as an artist." Marggy began to practice medieval design concepts and the growing of herbs in a small garden under the dining room window of her Ithaca home. "I made squares within squares, and I tried out plants that were used in medieval times."

One of the first projects that Marggy and the children, who by then were teenagers, tackled was building a lily pond. "We have been a close family; we have done everything together. Perhaps, in a way, that first lily pond was a memorial to my husband. It was an act of healing."

Seven years after the death of her husband, Marggy met Bob, a widower with one son, Ronald. Marggy and Bob had been exhibiting at the same gallery in Ithaca; they had known each other's work and reputation but had never met. After an eleven-week courtship, the couple married, combining the two families into "one warm, wonderful unit."

Following their move to Long Island, Marggy began to work on the design of the Springs garden, perfecting the geometric proportions of each element. When ready to build, Marggy called upon her sons, who spent the summer working with her. Since none of the family had ever laid brick, Marggy enlisted the help of a semiretired stonemason, Vernon "Bud" Greene, who came for a few hours in the cool of the early morning. Marggy's son Garry became Bud's apprentice, quickly mastering the skills, and with youthful energy worked all day. Her other son, Blake, wore the carpenter's apron and built the fence to Marggy's specifications. Meg, Marggy's daughter, later followed suit, as mason's assistant. Together, the two women prepared six brick rugs for an exhibition.

The side yard became a temporary outdoor studio. Bricks arrived by the truckload. A professional masonry wet saw was installed, but because of the noise it made, the studio was moved to an industrial space in nearby Amagansett. Later, to accommodate the work and Marggy's desire to remain at home, she designed and built a new studio to harmonize with the existing buildings.

Marggy's attention to patterning carries over her garden's design. She uses several visual devices in addition to the patterns created by the brick floor. She makes slight changes in

BELOW: **During the summer months a recirculating fountain runs constantly in the lily pond. Goldfish populate the pool, darting between the white water lilies. Marggy chooses both day and evening varieties, so that no matter the time of day, lilies are in bloom.** BOTTOM: **The plants Marggy has chosen were traditional to gardens in the Middle Ages. A 5-foot-tall mullen (***Verbascum thapsus***) glows in the early-morning light.**

UP AGAINST THE WALL
Espaliered Pears

STATELY ESPALIERED pear trees preside over Marggy's garden. Gifts from her children in 1987, they are now mature plants, meticulously pruned works of art.

Marggy purchased four types of espaliers: a six-armed palmette verrier, two single vertical cordons, two double horizontal cordons, and one single-U form, which she playfully joined at the top to form the shape of a pear leaf. The trees are varied as well, and it is essential to have different varieties so that they will cross-pollinate. The varieties she chose are 'Clapp's Favourite', 'Bartlett', 'Beurré d'Anjou', and 'Moonglow'. All are dwarf, as they grow one-half to one-third as tall as standards. Dwarfs bear fruit at about three years and are easier to train, to prune, and to pick. Their fruit is generally larger and better flavored than that produced by a standard-size tree.

The trees are trained against wires, which are attached to the fence and house by 8-inch eye-hooks. Marggy keeps the branches 4 to 6 inches away from the house and fence, as air circulation prevents disease. She ties the branches with gardener's twine, which she replaces each year. She maintains the six-armed palmette verrier and the single vertical cordons that flank it against the wall of the house at 7½ feet. The double horizontal cordons, which are trained against a fence, top out at 4 feet.

Marggy prunes the trees "religiously" three times a year—in mid-June, mid-July, and mid-August. Pears bear fruit on spurs, a twig or shoot that is contorted in shape and less than 6 inches long. Normally, a shoot is over 6 inches long, straight, and rapid-growing, with less concentration of leaves than what is produced on a spur. When the tree has reached its desired height, the shoots should be removed to induce blossom and spur formation.

"These trees, which flower in white in the spring and produce more fruit every summer, give me pleasure all year long," Marggy says.

BELOW: **A detail from one of Marggy's carpets demonstrates a complex patterning of brick. She incorporates both the smooth top and bottom surfaces with the rougher side faces, as each reflects light differently. The carpets usually do not have whole bricks in them because Marggy feels working with small pieces opens up so many more design possibilities.** BELOW RIGHT: **A 29-foot-long brick "runner" connects the Rug Garden to the house, where glass doors provide access to the living quarters and the studios.**

grade by using steps of varying heights. She planned the beds as squares and rectangles of various sizes extending into the paved area, rather than just skirting the perimeter.

The soil in Marggy's garden is hospitable to herbs. Neutral, sandy loam, which she amends with truckloads of composted cow manure and peat, is also well drained. Due to its north-south orientation the garden provides hot, dry areas for the gray-leafed Mediterranean plants like rue, lavender, clary sage, and lamb's ears. Well-chosen trees create more shaded beds for hellebores, trout lilies, trillium, mayapple, and columbine.

Margaret Kerr's herb collection—often containing 150 to 200 varieties—includes perennials, biennials, annuals, and bulbs. She encourages self-seeding plants like centranthus (*C. ruber*), which she saw growing in walls in England, honesty (*Lunaria annua*), and flax (*Linum usitatissimum*), "which can disappear for years at a time." Germander and lavender are used as low hedges. Tender perennials such as rosemary (*Rosmarinus officinalis*) and sweet bay (*Laurus nobilis*) grow in pots. Marggy's well-worn copy of *Sweet Herbs and Sundry Flowers,* which includes the Cloisters' plant lists, is filled with her terse notations: next to *Viola tricolor,* "Seeds itself in brick," and by *Physalis alkekengi,* "Took out."

Herbs, by their nature, are modest plants. They provide few blasts of color and rarely boast gigantic foliage or throw superstar tantrums. But either singly, like a dignified mother superior, or in profusion, like a procession of nuns, these plants have a quiet, unforgettable power. Their histories, many of which are cloaked in lore, make them seem venerable; they have earned respect. The orange fritillarias (*F. imperalis*) may be the most brilliant, and the pure white Madonna lilies (*Lilium candidum*) the most majestic. Marggy also speaks fondly of more diminutive plants, like the perky *Viola tricolor,* Johnny-jump-up, drawings of which are scattered throughout the margins of many medieval manuscripts. "How can a plant be happier or more delicate than that?"

Marggy reflects, "A new garden is a plink-plank-plunk place. You put in three or five of a particular plant. Then, over time, the plants grow together, and the place becomes a garden. Then, over much more time, the garden begins to have a mind of its own. To me, that's when the miracles happen."

Bob Richenburg, Marggy's husband, assembles gardens of stones collected on the couple's travels. Carefully chosen and placed, their spare arrangements add to the contemplative nature of the garden. Bob is not a gardener, but he is an "avid appreciator" of Marggy's work. In summing up his response to the spirit felt in gardens around the house and studios, Bob says, "Marggy has created our Paradise."

PATTERN AND FORM
Brick Carpets in the Landscape

ONE SIDE OF Margaret Kerr's 20-by-32-foot soundproof studio is a solid glass wall facing the meadow and the harbor. The building is both poetic and practical—a place to study and dream and a place to work. Brick works in progress are spread out on the floor and hang on the walls. Marggy says, as she turns a brick fragment in her hands, "I have a real passion for this material."

The floor of the studio is marked off in a grid, so that Marggy can play at laying out intricate brick patterns, including fringe, kilim bands, and borders, until they satisfy her. Some are prayer rugs with traditional *mihrab,* a pointed house-like or door-like configuration. Marggy never makes drawings; she prefers to begin to work and "let things happen."

Marggy installed a combination of skylights and metal halide lamps, which provide an accurate view of the subtle differences of color in brick. Dozens of milk crates and empty Sheetrock buckets contain precisely cut pieces of brick in every geometric shape imaginable. The natural variations that occur within one palette of bricks hark back to the differences in dye lots, a phenomenon called abrash, that occurs within a tribal carpet.

The smaller rugs are assembled in welded steel frames that resemble cookie sheets for a giant's kitchen. Holes for drainage are drilled in a grid in the bottom of the frame. The surface is then covered with landscape cloth to prevent the sand, the next layer, from leaking out. Then the bricks are placed in their prescribed pattern. Sand is thrown on the top, filling the crevices. "When you brush the sand off the top, it looks

as if you have just uncovered something thousands of years old. The rug instantly becomes ancient." The finished piece is forklifted onto a truck bed and moved to the place of installation.

Larger rugs are assembled on site. If outdoors, a bed of stone dust topped with sand is repeatedly compacted to a depth of about 6 inches to form a base; the edges of the rug are cemented into place. If indoors, the brick rug is installed with the preparations that would be given to laying a stone floor. A recent commission—a garden room's carpet measuring 9 by 26 feet, containing 2,420

pieces, and weighing 3 tons—took Marggy and her crew a week to install.

Marggy says that, unlike the artwork she did prior to her brick period, brick cutting and the final execution and installation of brick rugs are collaborative works. The two diamond-blade wet saws, where the bricks are precision-cut to her specifications, are operated by professional stonemasons, the indispensable brothers Joe and Candido Goncalves, in her studio. "I don't get near those saws," she says, "but, oh, do I love the sound of them in operation."

TREE-TRUNK TOPIARY

Richard Reames
Williams, Oregon

AT THE ENTRANCE to Richard Reames's garden, a simple wooden gate swings open to reveal a pair of quaking aspens, slim, creamy-barked trees that are in training to take the shape of the moon. Spread wide at the sides and joined at the top, they form a huge oval that beckons to travelers. A grassy path leads to a stream, where six hybrid poplars, lying on their sides and rooted to one bank, form a natural footbridge. On the other bank they are divided and joined to make a doorway. This strange and marvelous place is the studio of arborsmith Richard Reames, a sculptor whose medium is living trees. Says Richard, "You start by making two trees into one, and then see that the possibilities of bringing trees together are unlimited."

Richard's passion for training trees into fences, furniture,

"Communication with trees is a very slow thought—like conversation. Slowly, telepathically, the answer will come over time."

PREVIOUS PAGES, LEFT: **Richard Reames's cat Angel steps through the Moon Gate, an 8-by-5-foot oval opening.** RIGHT: **As the trees of the 7-foot-long footbridge grow in girth, they will form a solid floor. The trees are not rooted on the far side, as they might abandon the bridge portion to concentrate on sending nutrients the shorter distance from the new roots to the crown.** THIS PAGE, ABOVE: **The Reameses' log home.** OPPOSITE: **In a project for the Siskiyou Rare Plant Nursery located in nearby Medford, Richard used red alder to create a living bench. A total of twenty trees, sixteen for the front legs and four for the back, were planted, shaped, and grafted together. The two main trunks in the back will be grafted together next, and the rest will follow, ultimately joining all twenty trees into one trunk above the bench.**

dwellings, and other objects is relatively new; he has been at it for less than a decade. As a young man he traveled around the country, working at odd jobs as he needed them. "I lived light in those days," he recalls. When Richard reached his thirties he joined a group of friends, artists, and craftspeople who had chosen to live in harmony with the earth in the fertile Applegate River valley in southern Oregon. Framed by the pointed peaks of the Siskiyou Mountains, the area is rich in natural resources and history.

When glaciers covered most of the Northern Hemisphere, the east-west orientation of the Siskiyou Mountains presented a barrier. Glaciers flowed to the mountains' boundaries and then retreated, leaving the area's botanical heritage intact. The result is a great diversity in native plant species. The Zone 8 climate, where the ground does not freeze and the soil is rich, makes the valley a Mecca for horticulture businesses, from nurseries to vineyards.

With his wife, Maya Many Moons Reames, Richard staked his claim on a remote country road in the little town of Williams. In 1990 the couple acquired two acres facing west, where the evening sun sets behind the timbered mountains and kisses the fields with golden light. Pleased with their prospect, Richard, who had taken a college course in log house building, set about constructing a home. Over the next three years he built a two-story octagonal dwelling, 24 feet in diameter.

While he was erecting the third wall, the Reameses' daughter, Myray, was born. Becoming a father was a turning point for Richard, who realized he needed a career. "I prayed I would find something that was good for me and good for the earth," he recalls. As he sought his life's profession, images of the work of an uncelebrated eccentric named Axel Erlandson, a master of an art form that Richard has named tree-trunk topiary, began to haunt him. Richard had visited Erlandson's Santa Cruz Tree Circus (renamed Lost World by a subsequent owner) and had seen the fantastical spiral staircase, double heart weeping willow, 20-foot cathedral window, and needle-and-thread tree that Erlandson had created from the 1920s to the 1950s. As a child, Richard recalls, he was more interested in the dinosaurs than the trees. But he realizes now that the trees must have had a powerful effect on his subconscious. "One day I thought, 'Maybe I could do that.'"

Richard began to look closely at the trees in the forests around his home, imagining shapes and forms that he might create with them. For a while he worked in the wild on native trees such as firs and madrones. Drawing on his education in botany and biology,

BELOW: **Richard set eight white birch trees on 2½-foot centers around a circle to form a small, intimate room. It is especially beautiful in the fall, when the foliage turns a golden yellow.** BOTTOM: **To create a spiral tree, Richard planted two white birches a few inches apart and began the process of training them into a spiral form. A complete spiral occurs at about an 8-foot height. Since these are juvenile birch trees, their bark is still brown; it will turn white when the trees are about four years of age.**

Richard started to experiment with grafting techniques, primarily using the ancient practice of approach grafting.

At the same time he began to research the art of arbor sculpture, which he believes reached a zenith with Erlandson. To his disappointment, he discovered that Erlandson had been resolutely secretive about his methods; no records, other than a few local newspaper articles and a 1957 two-page spread in *Life* magazine, survive. But Richard was no stranger to pioneering, and he determined to teach himself. He returned to California to study Erlandson's surviving works and to pore over old photographs with a magnifying glass.

Often, rather than looking at a photograph's main subject, he concentrated on trees in the background, which could be seen in different photographs over a period of several years. In that way Richard was able to observe a tree's growth characteristics. For example, he saw evidence that the loops Erlandson had grafted in a tree were dying. He learned that "the tree's nutrients bypassed the loop in favor of a more direct nutrient route from root to crown." Thus he deduced that an "open-spaced design" ensures a higher success rate.

In creating arbor sculpture, Richard says trees can be planted as close together as the artist desires. "When they are joined through grafting, they essentially become a single tree with an extended root system." Symmetrical designs retain their balance, as they provide the tree with "equally distant pathways from root to crown." If a section becomes too large, a last-resort technique called ring barking, which entails removing a narrow strip of bark around a portion of the tree, or scoring, making *X* marks around the tree with a knife, will slow the tree's growth. These processes inhibit the movement of nutrients from the leaves through the phloem, the layer just under the tree's bark, to the roots.

For his living furniture, Richard says, "I look for trees that are supple in their youth, fast growers, have beautiful bark, and are disease-resistant." He claims almost any tree will work, except those that naturally lose their lower branches, and he is always testing new varieties. His current favorites are pin oak (*Quercus palustris*), a flexible, fast-growing oak with textural gray-and-white bark and bright yellow-and-red fall color, and white birch (*Betula papyrifera*), which is also very flexible and has distinctive white peeling bark.

A dozen nursery beds on Richard's property house thousands of saplings, which he calls his "art supplies." The nursery beds are oriented in a north-south direction so that the young trees don't cast shade on each other. To give his stock a boost, he supplements the clay loam with manure. The beds, ranging from one hundred to two hundred feet long, contain an ever-expanding and -changing collection of trees, including red alder (*Alnus rubra*), hybrid poplar (*Populus* 'Androscoggin'), Oregon Ash (*Fraxinus latifolia* or *F. oregona*), silver maple (*Acer saccharinum*), big-leaf maple (*Acer macrophyllum*), sycamore maple (*Acer pseudoplatanus*), larch (*Larix decidua*), golden willow (*Salix alba* var. *vitellina*), golden corkscrew willow (*Salix matsudana* 'Golden Curls'), sequoia (*S. sempervirens*), black locust (*Robinia pseudoacacia*), and cider gum (*Eucalyptus gunnii*).

When Richard starts a new piece, especially an abstract design, he makes a sketch to figure out the number and placement of the trees. Often the configuration of a tree's branches suggests a design. Several years ago at a Mother's Day sale, Richard purchased a sad specimen of a cherry tree in a pot. The leader had been broken off, resulting in six new branches' shooting out in different directions. He bent and grafted the branches into the shape of the Peace Sign, making it a living memorial to peace. Richard also takes an unusual approach to making tools—he grows trees through their handles, thus insuring that they are forever joined. For

example, he slipped a shovel head down over a hybrid poplar sapling. In a year and a half, the tree had grown to fill the handle, and the tree was cut from the ground.

Richard digs saplings and handles all bare-root material during their dormant season, mid-November through mid-March. He does much of the manipulation of the trunks—bending, twisting, weaving, turning—during the winter or early spring, when a plant is most supple. For the first few years the trees require wood or metal structural support, and that framework goes into place as the object is created. The size and configuration of the support are determined by the amount of stress the trees exert against their new shape. Over time, when the diameter, or caliper, of the tree matures, the supports can be removed. Chairs, for example, depending on the species of the tree, may need at least three years' growth to support the weight of an adult.

In creating a chair, Richard selects as many as ten similar saplings, divided between the two front legs, and two heavier ones, also matched in size, for the back. The front trees are woven to form the seat and the chair's back. At the points where they touch, they are grafted together; once the graft takes, the chair is exceedingly strong. The spaghetti-like roots of the five saplings that make up each of the front legs are gently intertwined, allowing the roots to

ABOVE LEFT: **A bench made of pin oak is planted in its traveling crate. For commissioned works, Richard prunes the leaves off the lower shaped areas to make the piece look more attractive. However, in his studio, he often permits the foliage, including the suckers, to remain on the tree so each leaf can act as a little solar panel, feeding the roots by photosynthesis. ABOVE: Situated in the middle of a path in Richard's studio, a chair of red alder grows out of the earth.**

ABOVE LEFT AND RIGHT: **The red alder house in Richard's studio is four years old; it is just one of the living houses that Richard is planting in this country and in Japan. Some structures are small and whimsical, like gazebos sited in clients' gardens; others are planted to become full-size houses, which, as the trees mature and become a solid wall, will receive second and third floors. Richard is convinced that living houses and living furniture are the "ultimate ecological solution. It's probably a little premature to think that you could live in these houses in the near future. Depending on the trees used it could take fifteen or twenty years for the trunks to grow together and form solid walls, but I think it could be done."**

continue to unite underground. Ultimately the dozen trees that make up a chair become like one. "The roots don't compete with each other; rather, they complement each other," Richard says. For a bench project the number of trees may be multiplied by three or four.

Richard prefers to plant a project in its final residing place, but that is not always practical. If a chair or bench is to be transported, Richard starts it in a container—a 25-gallon pot or a specially constructed box. He tries to move and plant the work during the winter months when the tree will be dormant and receive less shock to its system. To avoid sun damage to exposed trunks, he tries to install pieces facing north so the tree's foliage can shade its bare trunks.

For a gazebo or a fence, Richard favors the diamond pattern, often used in creating traditional Belgian fences, both for its beauty and for its structural stability. Richard plants his trees closer together, making the diamond pattern tighter. Of the hybrid poplar fence in his studio, Richard says he believes it will be a solid structure in seven years from the time it was planted. "That will certainly keep the deer out," he jokes.

From seats and fences, Richard has progressed to ever larger plantings. For a Fruit Room, Richard trained fifteen semidwarf cherries, pears, apples, and plums in an espaliered fashion. He tied their branches to horizontal wires and formed the door arch with pruned branches covering a metal form. When mature, the trees will be a solid wall, and as they become taller, he will direct them to join overhead. Richard plans to add grapevines to cover portions of the ceiling. "Imagine sitting there and reaching up to pick a plum or a grape," he muses.

A 22-foot circular Living House resides in one corner of the outdoor studio. For it Richard planted seventy-seven red alders 11 inches apart because, he says, "I liked the balance of the math." The tops of the trees are bent toward the center and wired together at the apex. Those leaders are attached to a central pole to give the trees support in the formative years. As they mature, he will graft the trees together, and like his other sculptures, the resulting tree will reach skyward, growing taller and taller.

Richard placed the doorway, an opening that curves around itself like the beginning of a spiral, on the lee side of the house opposite the prevailing southwestern winds so that "the cold winds will never blow through the door." To test window styles, he installed a metal-framed window, a wood window, and a window formed out of the trees themselves. Over time—he estimates as little as seven years for this house—the trees will form a solid wall. To be able to create livable living homes is one of Richard's goals. "We are moving closer to making truly habitable living structures."

When looking at his work, people often ask, "Doesn't this hurt the tree?" Richard believes the answer is no. "I am helping the tree take a form that is unique, astounding, and attractive to people. The tree gets a lot of attention, and it likes that." Richard points out that in nature trees often graft to each other and, in essence, give each other support. "It cannot hurt to have a little human intervention. When you look at a successful graft, you see the trees healed and joined together in perfect unity. Two trees—or more—will become as one."

BELOW LEFT: **To create the Faucet Tree, RICHARD drilled a ¼-inch hole through a hybrid poplar tree. He pushed the pipe through the hole and screwed on the faucet. Eventually, as the tree grows in girth, the pipe at the back will disappear into the tree.** RIGHT: **To make the birch shape around the Cello Window, Richard topped the tree's leader off at the right height; two branches on the side of the tree began to grow to replace the lost leader. Using U nails to secure the leaders, as the new pair of leaders grew, he trained them around a cello frame, which he had found at a yard sale.**

WHEN TWO BECOME AS ONE
Richard Reames's Grafting Technique

THE KEY to successful arbor sculpture, says Richard Reames, is the graft that takes. The joining of two plant stems is an ancient art and a common practice in the field of horticulture. By forcing a scion, or a cutting from one plant, to grow on the rootstock of another variety, the arborsmith unites the best characteristics of both in a single plant.

Richard notes that "the more closely related the tree species, the more successful the grafts." For example,

between the cambium layers. The cut surfaces of the stems are brought together and the two stems are bound together with stretch ties." The cambium layer, just a few cells deep, is located under the tree's bark. When the wounds in the cambium layer heal, the two trees have mated for life.

Richard cautions that a high-quality grafting knife with a sharp straight-edged blade is essential. He favors a knife with a handle and interchangeable blades, which

grafting one variety of an apple to another is a routine procedure, whereas grafts outside a species are possible but much more difficult to achieve.

Richard practices a technique known as approach grafting, which has a high success rate. "Two self-sustaining trees, or portions of a tree, are wounded and secured together, allowing a graft to form as the wounds heal," he explains. While approach grafting theoretically can be done at any time during the year, the best results are achieved in early spring when the tree is going through its most rapid growth cycle.

In his book *How to Grow a Chair: The Art of Tree Trunk Topiary,* Richard describes the approach grafting method: "Two stems of approximately the same diameter are used. . . . At the point where the two stems will be joined, remove a slice of bark and wood from each stem. The cuts should be the same size so that the cambium patterns, when joined, will match. Also, the cuts should be smooth and flat, enabling close contact

can be replaced when they grow dull. Since it is easy to spread infection or disease in the wound, Richard cleans his grafting tools religiously in a diluted bleach dip, approximately one part bleach to fifty parts water, and then rinses them in clean water.

Richard binds the graft as tightly as possible, ensuring that there will be no movement of the joined trees by wind. Plastic ties stretch as the tree grows, preventing the ties from cutting into the tree. Light-colored ties, like the green ones sold by the tree industry, reflect the solar heat. Richard periodically checks the progress of the graft and, if necessary, reties it to prevent constriction. As an additional protective measure, he wraps other parts of the tree that have been exposed through pruning and shaping with white tree bandage or paints them with tree paint to prevent those areas from being sunburned. A graft can become permanent as quickly as two months, "or it can take a season or three," says Richard. "Nothing in nature is so specific."

ROMANCE IN THE RUINS

Genevieve Munson Trimble and Morrell Feltus Trimble
St. Francisville, Louisiana

ON A STEAMY August day in 1972 Genevieve and Morrell Trimble
drove from New Orleans to Natchez. As was their habit, they slowed
down as they passed the iron gates to Afton Villa, the site of an
antebellum plantation a few miles north of St. Francisville, Louisana.
Both had always loved the great Gothic Revival mansion, now a
burned-out ruin, that stood at the end of an oak-lined avenue.

The Trimbles knew the house had burned to the ground in the
early 1960s, but the romantic image of the turreted edifice and its
celebrated gardens was a fixture in their memories. Morrell had
recently flown over the property and reported to Genevieve that
the place was "utterly desolate, the gardens a tangled thicket." That
August afternoon the gates happened to be open. On a whim, the
Trimbles drove slowly, sadly, under live oaks festooned with Spanish

Genevieve M. Trimble

"A new project starts the adrenaline going."

Morrell F Trimble

PREVIOUS PAGES AND ABOVE:
Genevieve and Morrell Trimble have spent the last three decades restoring the gardens of Afton Villa. Genevieve stresses the importance of focal points, and adheres to the tradition of placing statues and other ornaments in formal gardens. A marble statue of Flora graces the center of the maze, always holding a skirtfull of camellias. A stone basket with fresh flowers is an accent in the Ruins Garden.

moss, to view the gardens' condition up close. They saw that vines and briers had gained a stranglehold on the remaining azaleas and camellias. The boxwood parterres were overgrown and shaggy; their paths impassable. The wide steps that had once welcomed silk-slippered ladies to the ballroom now led to nothing. "It was a snake pit," recalls Genevieve.

These days, however, spring bursts forth at Afton Villa with 8,000 tulips, 13,500 pansies, 5,000 impatiens, and masses of petunias and pelargoniums within the crumbling brick foundation walls and the elegant surrounding gardens. A ravine at the lower end of wide lawns shimmers with the brilliance of 100,000 daffodils.

But on that evening a quarter of a century ago the couple could not erase the tragic image of the once grand plantation from their minds. Morrell observed, "It's just a matter of time before a developer levels the site and builds a subdivision." Genevieve, gardening instincts ignited, responded, "Wouldn't it be wonderful if someone cared enough to restore those gardens?"

Morrell reached for the phone and found that Afton Villa was on the market. He recalls, "We put in a bid by telegraph, and we owned it the next day—an overgrown garden, 250 acres, and no place to hang our hats."

"We had no idea what we were getting ourselves into," says Genevieve as she surveys the transformation the couple has wrought on 40 acres of the property. "We had no magic wand. It was a long, slow process, and we doubted our sanity more than once."

Three gardeners, led by Ivy Jones, work with Genevieve. "I was hired for two weeks, and I've been here twenty-six years," Ivy says with a laugh. In wry understatement, he notes, "We've had our headaches," but adds, "when it looks like it does today, it's all worth it."

Genevieve makes a distinction between a strict restoration, like Colonial Williamsburg or Monticello, and the Trimbles' own approach to preservation-conservation. "This garden, 150 years old, retains the imprint of several gardeners who have loved it and placed their signatures on it. It has the layers of time, of evolution, and we have honored that quality. We have looked to the spirit of the garden to guide us in our work. This philosophy allows us to beautify, enhance, even superimpose our own ideas, always maintaining the original footprint of the house and garden."

David Barrow, a descendant of the original family that settled the Afton Villa property, was the plantation's owner in the mid–nineteenth century. A widower and one of the country's

wealthiest cotton planters, he met and married beautiful young Susan Woolfork in 1847.

David gave Susan carte blanche to create her dream house and she determined to replicate a French Gothic chateau the couple had seen on their European Grand Tour honeymoon. The L-shaped forty-one-room house, built of cypress and stucco, was begun in 1849; the house and its extensive pleasure gardens took eight years to complete.

Dozens of live oaks (*Quercus virginiana*) were planted in two parallel lines to create an avenue with a dense, cathedral-like effect overhead. The 190-foot-long parterres, which included a maze, were laid out below the house. Additional gardens stretched in seven descending terraces, terminating above a ravine. Extensive flower and rose collections flourished on each terrace. The plantation was christened Afton Villa to celebrate the family's favorite song, "Flow Gently, Sweet Afton," frequently performed by David's daughter, Mary.

OPPOSITE: **The 150-year-old live oaks along the curving avenue are now over 60 to 70 feet tall. With hundreds of**

During the Civil War, the fortunes of the Barrow family were drastically reversed. With few to tend them, the plantation and its gardens deteriorated rapidly. In the latter part of the nineteenth century Afton Villa operated as a girls' school for twenty-five years, and in the twentieth century two successive owner-gardeners tried to restore the old gardens before fire destroyed the house in 1963.

When the Trimbles began their stewardship in the 1970s, the first task they tackled was chopping out the strangling vines along the live oak avenue and in the parterres. They removed over four hundred truckloads of debris that first winter. Along the curving half-mile entrance they cleaned out and pruned southern indica type azaleas—red 'Pride of Afton', named for the variety found on the property, hot pink 'Pride of Mobile', intense pink 'Rosedown Pink', magenta 'Formosa', and the wild pink-to-white Piedmont azalea (*R. canescens*)—a job that can be accomplished only in the cold months when Louisiana's resident snake population is in hibernation.

The Grand Staircase, an axial line that leads from the parterres down through the terraces, was restored next. New rose-colored gravel paths, complementing the brick of other walkways, were constructed where the original ones had been located. Ignoring the ruins "because they were just too overwhelming," the Trimbles concentrated on restoring the parterres. Slowly, they rejuvenated the boxwoods (*Buxus microphylla*), a glowing shade of chartreuse, in the serpentine beds and the maze. The plants that remain are typical of a nineteenth-century southern garden: fragrant tea olive (*Osmanthus fragrans*); banana shrub (*Michelia figo*); camellias, both *C. japonica* and *C. sasanqua;* and hydrangeas.

In 1979 the Trimbles were at last ready to tackle the ruins. They engaged Dr. Neil Odenwald, ASLA, former director of the School of Landscape Architecture at Louisiana State University, and the three of them began a joyful collaboration that continues to this day, as each new stage is initiated and executed.

azaleas in bloom in the early spring, the effect is of going back in time to enter an enchanted world. The maze of clipped boxwood hedges, TOP, makes a crisply architectural contrast to the unstructured, soft planting in the Ruins Garden, ABOVE.

COLOR WITHOUT END

Afton Villa Ruins Garden
Perennials and Annuals

BOTANICAL NAME	COMMON NAME	FLOWER COLOR	BLOOM TIME AND TYPE
Ageratum houstonianum	Ageratum	Blue	Spring to frost, annual
Ajuga reptans	Ajuga	Blue	Spring to frost, perennial
Alocasia species	Elephant ear	Green with purple stems	Spring to frost, perennial
Amsonia tabernaemontana	Amsonia	Light blue	Spring, perennial
Antirrhinum majus	Snap dragon	White, pink, red, yellow	Spring to early summer, annual
Artemisia ludoviciana	Artemisia	Gray, lacy foliage	Spring through fall, perennial
Caladium bicolor (bulb)	Caladium	White, 'Candidum'	Spring to fall, annual
Catharanthus roseus	Periwinkle, vinca	Pink, white, rose	Summer to frost, reseeding annual
Cleome hasslerana (*C. spinosa*)	Cleome	Lavender, white	Summer to frost, reseeding annual
Delphinium ajacis (*Consolida orientalis*)	Larkspur, 'Rabbit Ears'	Blue, purple, pink	Spring to early fall, annual
Delphinium grandiflorum	Delphinium	Blue, purple	Spring to early summer, annual
Dianthus deltoides	Dianthus, pinks	Pink, rose, white	Spring to summer, perennial
Digitalis purpurea	Foxglove	Cream, rose, pink-spotted throat	Spring to summer, biennial
Gerbera jamesonii	Gerbera daisy	Salmon, cream, white, yellow, orange	Spring to summer, perennial used as an annual
Hemerocallis fulva	Daylily	Apricot, yellow, orange	Late spring to early summer, perennial
Hosta species	Hosta, plantain lily, 'Royal Standard', 'Honeybells'	White, lavender	Summer, perennial
Hymenocallis caroliniana	Spider lily	White	Spring, perennial
Impatiens wallerana	Impatiens	Multicolors: pink, purple, red, salmon, white	Spring until frost, annual
Iris × *albicans*	White flag	White	Early spring, perennial
Iris × *germanica*	Bearded iris	Yellow, blue, purple, white, bronze	Midspring, perennial
Iris 'Louisiana'	Louisiana iris	Blue, white, bronze	Midspring, perennial
Lantana camara	Lantana	Yellow, white	Summer to frost, perennial
Lantana montevidensis	Lantana	Lavender	Summer to frost, perennial
Lathyrus odoratus	Sweet pea	White, purple, pink, red	Spring, annual
Leucojum aestivum (*L. vernum*)	Snowdrops, snowflakes	White tipped with green	Early spring, perennial
Lycoris radiata	Lycoris, spider lily, naked lady	Bright pinkish red	Autumn, perennial

Mentha spicata	Common mint	Green	Spring to frost, perennial
Mirabalis jalapa	Four o'clock	Bright pink, white	Summer to fall, perennial
Narcissus jonquilla	Jonquil	Yellow	Early spring, perennial
Narcissus tazetta	Narcissus	White	Early spring, perennial
Nicotiana alata	Flowering tobacco	White, cream, maroon	Summer, annual
Odontonema strictum	Fire spike	Bright red	Late summer to frost, perennial
Orthosiphon stamineus	Cat whiskers	White, blue	Summer to frost, annual
Pentas lanceolata	Pentas	White, pink	Spring to frost, perennial
Petunia × hybrida	Petunia	Pink, lavender, purple, white	Spring to summer, annual
Phlox divaricata	Spring phlox	Lavender to purple	March–April, perennial
Phlox paniculata	Summer phlox	Bright magenta	Summer to fall, perennial
Portulaca grandiflora	Portulaca, moss rose	White, rose, yellow, peach	Summer to fall, annual
Salvia elegans	Salvia	Pale blue	May through October, perennial
Salvia farinacea	Blue sage	Dark blue	May through October, perennial
Salvia guaranitica	Anise sage	Dark blue	May through October, perennial
Salvia splendens	Scarlet sage	Red	May through October, perennial
Scaevola aemula	Blue wonder	Bluish purple	Spring through fall in pots, annual
Tagetes spp.	Marigold	Yellow, orange	Late spring through fall, annual
Torenia fournieri	Torenia	Purple, pink, lavender	Spring through frost, reseeding annual
Tulbaghia violacea	Society garlic	Lavender-white	Spring to fall, perennial
Tulipa gesnerana	Tulip, 'White Triumphator', 'Golden Oxford', 'Monte Carlo', 'West Point', 'Mount Tacoma', 'Maureen', 'Ivory Floradale'	White, yellow	Spring, annual
Verbena × hybrida	Verbena 'Homestead Purple'	Lavender, purple	Late spring or early summer through fall, perennial
Veronica species	Veronica 'Icicle'	White	Spring through summer, perennial
Viola tricolor	Pansy	Blue, white, yellow, purple	November to mid-April, perennial
Zinnia elegans	Zinnia	Multicolors: red, white, orange, lavender, yellow	May to frost, annual

BELOW: **The original steps to the parlors and a ballroom, which once felt the brush of dance slippers, lend evocative charm to the Ruins Garden. The stairs all hold changing displays of potted flowers, like daffodils underplanted with pansies. Throughout the garden Genevieve repeats planted combinations in multiples, a powerful design device.**

The Ruins Garden covers about three-quarters of an acre on several levels. Genevieve admits that she secretly wished for Greek columns, "worthy ruins." For some years she did not see the potential beauty in her own brick walls, which were the foundations of a house, not of the Parthenon or a palace. However, after having visited the remains of castle walls used to brilliant effect at Sissinghurst Castle Gardens, Vita Sackville-West and Harold Nicolson's garden in Kent, England, she thought, "We have our own ruins. Let's see what we can make of them." Morrell and Neil concurred.

Slowly, as more tons of debris were removed, the foundation walls and a series of steps were revealed. Genevieve left the volunteer trees, particularly the tallow (*Sapium sebiferum*) to cast shade. The wisteria was brought under control, but allowed to drape extravagantly from trees and stairways. Clipped and shaped cherrylaurel (*Prunus caroliniana*) is used as a screen and in large planters.

The Trimbles welcome guests, often serving lunch to a score or two on cloth-covered tables, each with its own bouquet, in the Ruins Garden. Always civic-minded, they also host benefit events for their favorite charities and organizations, like the Southern Garden Symposium or the Garden Conservancy. The Afton Villa Gardens are open to visitors six months of the year, in the spring and fall. Undeterred by visitors, ducks, geese, and an unpredictable peacock named Rex, in honor of Morrell's tenure in 1980 as King of the New Orleans Mardi Gras, roam the garden. Genevieve says that people and animals bring "animation" to a garden. "They are what makes it come alive."

Genevieve keeps a detailed garden diary, now in its third volume, to which she refers while

making decisions for the upcoming seasons. "Those records are crucial," she says. For example, while she has experimented with many tulip varieties, she says the yellow 'Monte Carlo' and the white 'Mount Tacoma' (both peony types), the 'Ivory Floradale', 'White Triumphator', 'Maureen' (single whites), and 'Yellow Oxford' and 'West Point' (single yellows) outperform the rest. Genevieve cautions that after they bloom the tulips must be pulled out, bulb and all. If left through the heat of deep summer, the bulbs can cause soil-related diseases, such as botrytis blight or rhizoctonia, which would necessitate replacing all the soil in an infected bed. Hundreds of delphiniums, petunias, plumbagos, and verbenas are tucked into the holes left by the spent tulips. Such intense planting takes its toll on the soil; in order to keep the garden fertile, soil is replaced on a staggered schedule every three years.

ABOVE: **Genevieve uses masses of a single flower, like white impatiens, to fill parterre beds.** BELOW: **The Ruins Garden, designed for ebullient color all season, require extensive annual plantings. The original color schemes of the house interior—yellow, white, lavender, and blue—became Genevieve's palette. Since the Trimbles had visited the house in its glory, Genevieve was able to recall the locations and colors of all the rooms, noting that one flight of steps led to the Yellow Parlor, and another to the Blue Parlor.**

100,000 DAFFODILS

The Best Choices for Naturalizing

NAME	COLOR	TIME OF BLOOM
'Carlton' (large-cupped narcissus)	Two-toned yellow, large cup	Mid- to late season
'Delibes' (large-cupped narcissus)	Large cup, golden perianth and shallow, bowl-shaped crown of yellow with orange rim	Midseason
'Fortune' (large-cupped narcissus)	Yellow perianth and yellow crown edged in red	Midseason
'Mount Hood' (trumpet daffodil)	A trumpet daffodil that opens creamy yellow and gradually turns ivory white	Midseason
'Papyraceuns' (paper-white narcissus)	A traditional favorite in the Gulf area; a wonderful naturalizer with fragrant white flowers	Early; February at Afton Villa
'Silver Charms' (Tazetta narcissus)	Six or more flowers per stem, silvery perianth with a yellow cup crown, dark green foliage	Mid- to late season
'Thalia' (Triandrus, the orchid narcissus)	Three or more white flowers per stem with recurved petals and cup crown	Late season
'White Lion' (double narcissus)	Fragrant, creamy white, gardenia-like bloom with shorter yellow petal segments and a frilled double center	Midseason
'Yellow Sun' (trumpet daffodil)	Large, brilliant yellow perianth and yellow crown, resembles 'King Alfred'	Early

The last large area to be developed was the Daffodil Valley, an "eyesore" ravine with a stream that begged for Genevieve's imaginative touch. Several thousand daffodils have been planted each year. Plants indigenous to West Feliciana—the parish in which Afton Villa is located—have been introduced, including Grancy Grey-beard (*Chionanthus virginicus*), silverbell (*Halesia carolina*), tulip tree (*Liriodendron tulipifera*), winter honey-suckle (*Lonicera fragrantissima*), cow-cumber (*Magnolia macrophylla*), trillium

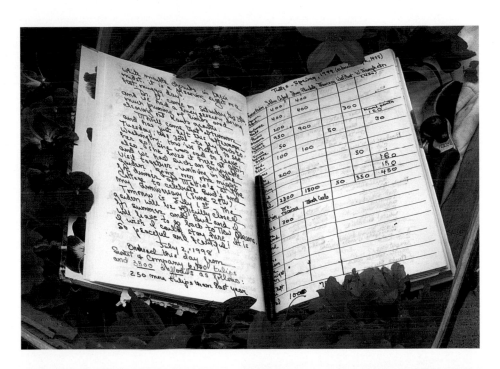

(*T. foetidissimum*), partridge berry (*Mitchella repens*), as well as several types of wild ferns.

"I never started out to be a restorer of gardens, but that's the course my life has taken," says Genevieve. She is constantly changing combinations, refining her ideas. "I'm such a dreamer. I'd like to plant all those terraces with perennial borders to replicate its nineteenth-century heyday. But I have learned the old lesson 'If you can't maintain it, don't have it.'" Another significant part of her public persona back in New Orleans is the presidency of the New Orleans Botanical Garden Foundation, and she excels at raising resources to restore the 1930s garden. Weekdays she visits prospective donors and writes proposals. Weekends are spent at Afton Villa, which is now on the National Register of Historic Places.

Genevieve reflects, "The gardens at Afton Villa literally rose out of the ashes. For me, they are symbolic of the Old South, of the enduring spirit of people and their ability to conquer all obstacles—a form of hope and faith."

Genevieve is a disciplined gardener who keeps detailed notes in her garden journal each season. Three volumes now comprise an archive of the progress of the garden's restoration. As a practical tool, they also ensure that successful plantings can be replicated in subsequent years. Genevieve believes these journals will be valuable to later generations as they seek information about the Trimble years in this glorious, historic garden.

CRAZY FOR COLOR

Michael W. Bowell
Malvern, Pennsylvania

"I GUESS my garden is a little like Shangri-la," observes plantsman, colorist, and artist Michael Bowell. Tropicals potted in oversize containers are the backbone of his daring perspective. "This is a garden always in flux," Michael continues. "However, I always plan the garden to reach its peak of performance in September and October, when many gardens are going to sleep. By then most perennials have finished their shows; annuals are tired and ragged. But the tropicals are merrily singing their hearts out."

Individual vignettes planted in massive 15- or 20-gallon pots line a warren of grass paths, each one as audacious as a stage set designed by Salvador Dalí or David Hockney. Tropical plants—canna, brugmansia, banana, solenostemon, palms, phormium, podocarpus, variegated ficus—are the stars, while waves of bold

Michael Bowell

"I love that crescendo of color at the end of the season."

natives, like Joe-Pye weed, purple coneflower, plume poppy, and ornamental grass, form the chorus line. Michael outlines the recipe for his sorcery: quantities of bold foliage, strong vertical lines, fountain effects from weeping plants and ornamental grasses, contrasting textures, and an understanding of color theory. Throw in a hint of wit and a dash of luck with weather conditions.

Each year the compositions are different, experimental. "My garden never looks the same from summer to summer. I get bored easily—I revel in change. I'm always fine-tuning, trying to make the garden more exciting," he explains.

When viewed from the road above, the main garden looks like a maze, but it does not have the orderly geometry of a maze in a formal European garden. Rather, paths in seemingly random patterns twist and turn to meet each other. It is easy to feel lost in this land of the Lilliputians, a sensation exaggerated by the potted plants and ornamental grasses that tower at the edges of the paths.

The lack of man-made architecture contributes to the garden's primeval quality. That absence of architectural reference makes the half-acre garden seem endless. The placement of plants creates the divisions; there is no sculpture, no Victorian urn or column fragment. Instead, a line of broom corn (*Panicum miliaceum*) forms one wall, a half-dozen dragon's eye pines (*Pinus densiflora* 'Oculus-draconis'), their needles edged in gold, another. Some background plantings follow straight lines; others undulate in sinuous curves. A young cut-leaf staghorn sumac (*Rhus typhina* 'Laciniata'), its branches outstretched, offers niches for tableaux.

Arbors, created from saplings or bent bamboo, are draped with lush, fast-growing vines, like the purple-flowering hyacinth bean (*Dolichos lablab*), the old morning glory stand-by *Ipomoea tricolor* 'Heavenly Blue', the tiny red-star-blossoming cypress vine (*Ipomoea quamoclit*), or *Solanum jasminoides* 'Album'. Arched forms seem to emerge from the earth without visible structure. They provide enticing doorways to successive openings; "rooms" would be too confining a term.

Michael admits that visitors often gasp at the color in his garden. "Many people compare plant combinations to paintings, but for me the analogy has always been to music. I want a full symphonic sound rather than a four-piece band. The sound from each instrument, when they are all played together, should add up to more than the individual horn or string." He grins as he allows, "I'm partial to the cymbals."

Color *is* what people see first, but he cautions that his initial considerations are shape and texture. "Elements must have contrast. If you have no contrast, you have no tension. If you have no tension, you have no rhythm." When he questions the effect of a composition, he

PREVIOUS PAGES, LEFT: **Michael Bowell's bold architectural forms are created with plants like water canna (*Thalia dealbata*) rather than with buildings.** RIGHT: **His dazzling display of tropical foliage and flowers—in chartreuse, magenta, coral, purple, yellow, flame, orange, and hot pink—splashes like a mirage across the rural landscape.** THIS PAGE, ABOVE: **An arbor smothered with the annual fast-growing (*Ipomoea alba*) divides one garden experience from another.**

TOP: **Michael includes a mini water garden in many of his scenes. Tucked off center, it provides asymmetrical interest on one side; its weight may be balanced by a tall plant like the miniature date palm (***Phoenix roebelinii***). Changing reflections in even the smallest amount of water "brings tropical associations."**
ABOVE: **A brilliant grouping that includes celosia, solenostemon, and lantana.**

photographs it in black-and-white. "Black-and-white tells the truth about how effective an arrangement is."

Then he thinks color. Michael often uses direct complementary colors: red and green, yellow and purple, orange and blue. He notes the power of accents; red is a stoplight against a field of green. When working with analogous colors, those next to each other on the color wheel, he "plays with intensities." A planting in mauve, lavender, and pale pink may be hit with a jolt of magenta or Pepto-Bismol pink. "You can add clear yellow, like *Canna* 'Canestoga' or the creamy yellow of *Phygelius* × *rectus* 'Moonraker', to almost anything for highlights. And a little chartreuse, like a hint of *Solenostemon* 'Line', *Carex stricta* 'Bowles' Golden', *Hedera helix* 'Goldchild', *Plectranthus* 'Lemon Lime', or *Ipomoea batatas* 'Margarita', is like upping the ante. It ties everything together." As for *Solenostemon:* "I couldn't garden without them. You never have to deadhead them or stake them. If it's hot they grow; if it's cool they're equally happy. They range in size from 8 inches to 5 feet, and their color range is endless."

Michael says that his passion for color probably began in the fourth grade, when his mother bought a couple of packages of zinnia and balsam seeds for him. "I planted the seeds in a cracked cement pot on our New Jersey patio, which overlooked the twelve lanes of expressway tying Atlantic City to Philadelphia. Our family left for vacation, and, when we returned, the patio was transformed by a mass of color. To me it was a miracle in the midst of all that concrete."

Michael's gardening urge quickly outgrew the single pot. In high school he caught the competitive bug when a neighbor took him to the Philadelphia Flower Show. Michael took to raising prize vegetables, and his blue-ribbon houseplants lined the family's windowsills. By college (Rutgers University), Michael was majoring in botany. "But even then," he recalls, "I did not see gardening as an artistic endeavor but rather as a scientific exercise." A wise counselor suggested that Michael think about transferring to horticulture, where his talent for design, as well as his interest in plant culture and management, could mature; it was the moment of epiphany.

Michael turned to nature to study design, analyzing the layering effects of tall trees, understory trees, shrubs, and ground covers that became "drop-dead compositions." From then on, through graduate school and the development of his profession as floral and garden designer, he has never questioned his calling.

In 1988 Michael bought a modest 5-acre parcel of land parallel to Pennsylvania's six-lane turnpike—hardly the most tranquil location. A first priority was to create a green wall of trees as a buffer against the noise. Then, he recalls, "I studied the shape of the land. I looked to exaggerate its differentials. Where it is tall, I made it taller; where it dips I made it deeper— all without the use of earthmoving machines."

To give the property bones, Michael planted drifts of trees—dogwoods, redbuds, bald cypresses, oxydendrums, sweet bay magnolias—by the dozens. "I didn't want the arboretum look of individual trees, but rather the continuity of masses throughout the garden." Walls in place, Michael planted carpets: 12,000 narcissus bulbs, joined by vast numbers of fritillarias, anemones, irises, and tulips. Hardy perennials were grouped in large plantings. "I filled the garden with blocks of texture and color," he says. Temporary plastic-covered hoop houses for nurturing his burgeoning collection of tropical plants were erected three years before he built his home.

Then came the unique vision, which must have rumbled for years under the surface, like the fire in the depths of a volcano. With logic, difficult to refute, Michael says, "Since the Pennsylvania climate is tropical in the summer, why not treat it like the tropics? So I think of it more as Southeast Asia or South America."

Thus, the hunt for brazen foliage began. With his arms outstretched in imitation of a golden *Hosta* 'Sum and Substance', Michael intones with a wink, "I'm a hosta, hear me roar."

BELOW: **As a permanent backbone for the masses of annual summer color, Michael uses elegant, gestural conifers, like Sargents's weeping hemlock (*Tsuga canadensis* 'Pendula').**
BOTTOM: **At the garden's center, a small pond, dug from a low, boggy area, mirrors the leafy canopy above. A view of a throng of water lilies, water hyacinths, and blue pickeral weed is framed by jewelweed,** *Impatiens capensis*, **and umbrella plant (***Cyperus alternifolius***). The eye reads expanse, yet the pond is only 30 feet wide.**

It was this attitude, but with a vertical, rather than horizontal, habit that Michael sought as accents for his garden, and he eventually found them in the form of cannas. These were followed by bananas (the green *Musa* × *paradisiaca,* the mottled *Musa zebrina,* and the red *Ensete*

In parallel beds along the entrance path, Michael repeats gold, copper, and chartreuse by using plants like *Lantana* 'Samantha', *Plectranthus* 'Lemon Lime', and *Solenostemon* 'Coppertone'. At the end of the season, annuals and tender perennials have grown so profusely in their containers that many of the pots are completely hidden from view; the effect makes the garden feel truly tropical.

ventricosum 'Maurelli'), gingers (*Hedychium coronarium*), and elephant ears (*Colocasia esculenta*).

A few hardy trees can hold their own in these arrangements. "A *Styrax obassia* has big wide leaves and *Magnolia macrophylla* looks tropical. It has the most enormous leaves of any tree hardy to this area. The juvenile tulip tree (*Liriodendron tulipifera*), which pops up all over this garden, has leaves five times the size of those of the mature tree. When the tulip trees get too big I cut them back to the ground or transfer them elsewhere." He adds, "I'm always on the hunt for hardy perennials—the tough characters, like the yucca, which I call the bromeliads of the garden because of its distinct architecture, particularly *Yucca flaccida* 'Golden Sword'. Or *Aruncus dioicus,* Japanese anemones, *Hosta plantaginea,* and lots of daylilies. No prima donnas. I don't have time to coddle the perennials."

The key to this high-spirited planting is winter planning—and protection. After all, winter underscores the reality of Pennsylvania geography with a chilling bang. Says Michael, "This garden appears for a few months and then disappears. Like that." He sends his large specimens—brugmansias, lantanas, hibiscus, fuchsias—into a state of "suspended animation." He cuts them back to "the main frame": the brugmansias by one-third, the fuchsias and lantanas, unless they are standards, by as much as 80 percent. He clips off the side branches and removes all foliage, then binds them to take up little space in their greenhouse winter quarters. He lays many on their sides and stores them under benches. "Then I run them on the dry side. When stowed on their sides they receive very little of the regular overhead greenhouse watering."

Michael digs up the cannas and stores their bulbs in stacked plastic bulb bins. He takes cut-

ABOVE: "The beauty of using non-hardy plants is that the combinations change constantly, making them much more dynamic," says Michael, indicating a pairing of *Solenostemon* 'Tapestry' and a flaming celosia. BELOW: The greenhouse is set on concrete sidewalls; its floor is 2 feet of gravel. The walls and ceiling are an acrylic material, chosen both for its diffused transmission of light and for its economy; it is reputed to be twice as efficient as glass in both winter and summer. The greenhouse, which has hot-water fin-tube heat, is divided into two sections: the main section is maintained between 58 and 65 degrees, but the second section, used in the winter primarily for plant storage, remains at about 50 degrees.

tings from solenostemon, plectranthus, salvias, and impatiens. The palms, while pruned, receive the royal treatment and become the backbones of winter greenhouse arrangements. Michael treats most plants with an ultrafine horticulture oil spray to prevent outdoor bugs from becoming inside pests.

The state-of-the-art 32-by-48-foot greenhouse, which replaced the hoop houses, is attached to the east side of Michael's barn-like house. Michael steps from his bedroom onto a second-floor balcony, which juts out into the greenhouse like the prow of a ship nosing into a tropical inlet. At a round table in the center of this perch Michael conducts winter business, part of which is to oversee his charges. His plants are "uncountable. Thousands, I guess." While side areas are ordered in shelved rows for raising the multitudes his garden demands, the center aisle is arranged for leisurely strolls to study specimens, from lady's slipper orchids to bromeliads in bloom, a little like a modern version of a Victorian conservatory. A bank of fluorescent lights lines the back wall, where seedlings start their lives. "It is a safe spot where they won't receive the brunt of the spray nozzle and be knocked out of their pots," Michael says. "We water this place like a bunch of wild firemen."

If Michael favors tropical plants, would it not make sense to move to a warmer climate? "Oh, no, I love all kinds of plants; I have to have them *all*. Diversity is the primary ingredient for an exhilarating diet," he responds. "After all, it's easier to heat a palm than it is to refrigerate a maple."

ARCHITECT OF COLOR

Michael Bowell Sets the Scene

LIVING VIGNETTES of riotously colorful plants are the defining feature of Michael's garden design, and he composes each one meticulously. "Of course, all rules are made to be mastered and then bent," Michael laughs. "That's where instinct and imagination take over. That's the freedom of play." And play he does, with bold combinations and dense planting. The 15- to 20-gallon pots hold as many as six to twelve different

plants. Michael thinks of each pot as a separate arrangement, which when added to the larger scene, reiterates his design.

To create a vignette, Michael begins with its structure. He looks for a plant with presence, a Pavarotti of the plant world: a tall, big-leafed textured character. "Once in its spot, it almost tells me what to add. The bronze canna with coppery blossoms (*C.* × *generalis*) that prompted this grouping, for example, has style."

Michael suggests that the simplest way to begin to lay out an arrangement is to think in terms of a loose triangle, placing the dominant plant in the center. Sometimes he sets this theme plant on an overturned pot to give it additional height. Other strong personalities flank the lead, often brought slightly forward to exaggerate their importance. To qualify for inclusion in such an arrangement, plants must either contrast

with or retell the theme. Michael chooses a banana to echo the canna's burgundy foliage and carry the color higher. A bronze cordyline—with a fountain of narrow spikes, rather than broad leaves—reinforces the motif.

Enter the supporting players, having passed their auditions based on the principles of balance, rhythm, proportion, and scale. A black bamboo (*Phyllostachys nigra*) offers delicate foliage in a darker hue. A *Buddleia asiatica* provides height, its lacy gray foliage setting off the hard edges of the canna, banana, and cordyline; its blue flowers are a foil for the intensity of the purple. As the summer progresses, the buddleia also fills empty spots. An unnamed hibiscus, *Lantana* 'New Gold', and impatiens are placed so as to mingle and fill crevices with added texture. The pinks and reds of *Fuchsia* 'Thalia', *Dahlia* 'Bishop of Llandaff', and pentas lend spots of color and harmony. Michael then sets the whole arrangement off with chartreuse (*Solenostemon* 'Line' and *S.* 'Wizard Golden'), the "life of the party."

Lush, overripe foliage, Michael's hallmark, is a result of a religious fervor toward feeding. "Would you forget to give your child a meal?" he asks. Each new potted tribe receives an application of a slow-release fertilizer (14-14-14, three- to four-month formula), then two additional "shots" at six-week intervals. A liquid fertilizer is applied at least every other week throughout the season. He alternates a balanced 20-20-20 with a 10-30-20 blossom booster.)

Watering a potted garden is a challenge, and the huge pots are Michael's nod to pragmatism. Besides providing grandeur in a small garden, like overscale furniture in a diminutive room, they retain moisture, so they need to be watered less frequently than smaller ones. Still, Michael must drag the hose, his only source of water, from tub to tub every other day in the dry heat of the summer. "I wouldn't grow plants in small pots. Who has the time? I do all this by hand, so my methods had better be practical as well as great fun."

PLANTS IN THE ARRANGEMENT

Canna × *generalis* (Unknown hybrid, a gift from a friend)

Buddleia asiatica

Ensete ventricosum 'Maurelli'

Phyllostachys nigra

Pentas lanceolata

Fuchsia 'Thalia'

Impatiens 'Celebration Bright Coral'

Dahlia 'Bishop of Llandaff'

Solanum rantonnetii

Solenostemon 'Line'

Solenostemon 'Wizard Golden'

Solenostemon 'Sabre Mix'

Hibiscus hybrid (unknown)

Lantana 'New Gold'

Cordyline australis 'Purpurea' (Bronze cordyline)

WIZARD OF WONDERLAND

Marcia Donahue
Berkeley, California

A LUSH TUNNEL of acanthus, bamboo, fuchsia, and azara hugs the side of Marcia Donahue's Victorian house. On the Fallen Leaf Path the flagstones are carved leaves, and iridescent or marbleized bowling balls define the edges of the borders. Glazed ceramic bamboo in orange and white mimics the real plant in shape, if not in color. The line is blurred between what nature has done and what Marcia—artist, sculptor, and gardener—has imposed. "I try to collaborate with my material, to keep my part low-key," she explains.

Found materials, like chimney flues and terra-cotta drainpipes, are attached to one another, sculpture assemblages that hint at other extraterrestrial realities. "Ideas just build on themselves," Marcia observes about the creation of this otherworldly place. "Experiencing the garden is like a treasure hunt for things not always

Marcia Donahue

"I look for extremes in texture, either very fine or very coarse."

easily seen. Details are revealed as you travel through the garden. What you see is up to you."

Ten years ago, Marcia, who majored in fiber art at the Massachusetts College of Art and had worked in laminated leather and wood for a number of years, turned to stone. She immediately began to carve pieces to go into her garden and in the intervening years her art and her gardening have fused into a single discipline. Many of the principles she used in creating textiles, she has translated into gardening. "They are closely related. Both are about texture, patterning, interweaving, color combinations, and the play of light."

Playful and decorative touches are everywhere. A cluster of 18-foot Italian cypresses, (*Cupressus sempervirens*), resemble corkscrews to heaven, each topped with an imaginary bird. A contorted larch (*Larix kaempferi* 'Diana'), decorated with pieces of California jade found on a beach near Big Sur, has year-round holiday glamour. A Victorian bathtub, piped for hot and cold water, sits on a raised platform in the shade of *Podocarpus nagi* and *Leptospermum ericoides*.

Perhaps most emblematic of Marcia's iconoclastic approach to garden design is her "wish-fulfilling stone," an elongated heart-shaped stone that lies on the Glass and Pebble Beach, a semicircle of gravel mixed with shards of brilliant-colored, stream-washed glass and stone fossils. "Finding that stone in a stream bed in Mendocino County was a dream. I changed it very little. Put both hands on it and make a wish," Marcia instructs. "After all, your own backyard belongs to you. You can do anything you want. You can, and I do."

Marcia and her former husband purchased the three-story 1890s fixer-upper on a quiet side street in Berkeley in 1978. As a child growing up in Marin County, north of San Francisco, Marcia had helped her mother garden, but this 40-by-60-foot backyard provided her with her first opportunity to create a garden of her own. Guided by artistic instincts, a penchant for risk taking, and a lively sense of humor, Marcia learned by doing. "This garden does have traditional elements, but perhaps they're not obvious because my garden may be more shamelessly personal than most."

To relieve the flatness of the typical city backyard, one of the first things Marcia did was to build a mound, which unconsciously reflects the mounts in medieval gardens. She laid out a pattern of paths, basically a figure eight with offshoot curlicues. "While it may seem like you have gone a long way, that you might be lost, in fact, you always come back to the beginning," she says. She erected cairns, traditional marking devices to keep people on course. Some are stacked stones that have been pierced and then threaded on pipe, "like shish kebab." Carved into Marcia's cairns are words like HERE and CAIRN, RIGHT PATH. She carved leaf masks that suggest the European tradition of the green man dressed in leaves and used as a decorative motif in architecture. She built follies, which hark to the "folk art" garden tradition but are stamped with her individualized, quirky view.

Marcia learned about plants—"a happy addiction"— accumulated voraciously, and she

PREVIOUS PAGES: **Behind a luxuriant facade of exotic plants, like** *Parkinsonia aculeata, Chorisia speciosa,* **and a hundred-year-old dracaena, sculptor Marcia Donahue (herself masked by a** *Trevisia palmata* **leaf) creates an environment in which making art and making a garden are a single pursuit.** THIS PAGE, OPPOSITE: **A monumental head, which Marcia carved from California golden granite, rests against a pillow of ivy,** *Hedera helix* **'California Gold'. It is surrounded by bamboo** *Phyllostachys heterocycla pubescens* **'Moso', chosen for its reference to old forests in Japan.** ABOVE: **Of her "wish-fulfilling stone" Marcia says, "The protuberances fill the hollow of the hands—for wishing."**

now has an encyclopedic collection. "I love plants that are astonishing, mad, and marvelous." Some plants are tiny treasures, like *Aristolochia fimbriata,* whose flowers seem to have eyelashes, but others boast big foliage and habit, like the black tree fern *Cyathea medullaris.* Clump-forming bamboos are particular favorites, and she has collected over twenty-five varieties, from the 2-foot *Pleioblastus viridistriatus* 'Chrysophyllus' to the 15-foot blue

TOP: **A carved granite tuffet, complete with piping and tassels, offers a resting spot, albeit a somewhat hard one, for Miss Muffet or a kneeling knight. Marcia's initial is carved in the center.** ABOVE: **Marcia, who "recycles everything," used bricks from the house's foundation to build a patio by the Handprint Pond.** RIGHT: **A stone poem playing with the same four letters, decorated with *Rosa* 'Erfurt', lies on the Glass and Pebble Beach.**

bamboo, *Drepanostachyum falcatum.* The garden has grown into a densely packed urban jungle.

Wherever Marcia travels she looks for stone—on beaches, in riverbeds, even along the highway. "People have been carving stone for so long. It is very satisfying to me to evoke those traditions, that history," she says. "My inspirations are varied. I have studied the stone works from many cultures, from those at Angkor Wat to the Olmec heads in Mexico to the serene figures of Buddha. I collect African sculpture and textiles. Visitors, who bring their own responses to my work, say 'Easter Island' or 'Angkor Wat.'"

An arbor, made of two cast-iron lampposts with capitals that suggest Adam and Eve, is smothered with kiwi vine *Actinidia deliciosa* (*A. chinensis*), both male and female plants. The vigorous vine "sends out arms easily 30 feet long." The arbor opens to a brick floor, where intermittent bricks are carved with the words WELL WELL WELL. Deadpan wit again: they cover the site of an old well. Baby tears (*Soleirolia soleirolii*) fills the cracks, like green liquid oozing up from regions below. Other ground covers, *Fuchsia procumbens,* with its upward-facing flowers and bright blue pollen, liriope, and several small bamboos are tightly woven to leave no empty niches.

On the other side of the miniature clearing is the Handprint Pond, which is 10 feet long. "A hand is the means by which you do all these things. Gardening, even when it tries not to look like it, is a human endeavor. So I thought a hand was an apt form." Marcia formed the shape— "You always have the model with you at the end of your arm," she observes wryly—like a basket using construction rebar for support, and then patted concrete into the sides and bottom. It offers peninsulas for planting. Water lettuce in soft celadon catches the dew. Glass balls, inspired by the net floats used by Japanese fishermen, which fascinated Marcia as a child, catch the light like bubbles on the water. A single electric wire surrounds the pool and is activated at night "to deter the invading raccoons from tearing the water lilies to shreds."

Stones are carved with words like ORNA MENTAL; MID LIFE CRISIS; WRIGHT WRITE RIGHT RITE. Marcia says, "Writing on a rock goes back to the beginning of time." Sometimes she chisels "mystery words" hidden in the veins of her carved oak leaves. "You could puzzle out what they say. But, more important, I just like the presence of language."

A carved skull lies on its side at the edge of the pond. Ceramic slugs and snails creep across it and up the nearby chimney flue toward a bowling ball and head at the top. Several tall ceramic bones, "Bone Boo," which lean akimbo, are amusing and eerie at once. Are they bones or are they bamboo? The Gravestone Path, which once led to the compost, is paved with sample stone monuments from a stone-cutting business that is now defunct. They were found at the dump, an endless source of inspiration. One gravestone says, "Marcia Rest in Peace." Trees like *Dacrydium cupressinum* and the blue *Cupressus torulosa* var. *cashmeriana* seem to weep. Steams of purple heart, *Setcreasea pallida,* cascade from the raised bed into the path. While Marcia says she is not particularly preoccupied with disease and death, "there are ample examples of both in every garden. Yet, happily," she adds, "the garden offers reminders of health and regeneration."

Inspired by shrines in Mexico, Marcia has given both death and life their own altars, just across the way from each other. Along a shady path stands a carved stone column, Sante Muerte. Opposite the mistress of death, a full-bosomed Sante Vida is a celebration of life. At her feet is a carved leaf loaf—bread from stone. Reaching over the goddesses' heads like a great protector stands the "blue-bottled Leptospermum tree." Skyy Vodka bottles, saved by a local bartender, are attached to the ends of the branches, like a new variety of bright blue flower. "Great color, aren't they?" asks Marcia. A bottle tree, a tradition that came to the South from the Congo, is a "little ancestor-appeasement device, which has become quite fashionable." One of the lower branches of the aged tea tree, which was planted by the previous owner, obstructs the path; the visitor is forced to "bow under the bough."

Rescued granite curbstones and pieces of old crockery form a "small Central American

TOP: **At Sante Muerte's feet, black candles burn and a stone is carved with the word** NAUGHT. **Key to the scene, a 2½-foot-tall** *Arisaema taiwanense* **with a zebra-striped trunk holds its foliage like an umbrella.** ABOVE: **The Gravestone Path, almost enveloped in suitably dark-colored vegetation, leads around the edge of the Handprint Pond.**

FASCINATING RHYTHM
(Mostly) Clump-Forming Bamboos

"HOORAY FOR *the giant woody grasses,*" *says* Marcia. *Except as noted in italics, these are hardy to 0°F.*

PLANT NAME	HEIGHT	DESCRIPTION
Bambusa multiplex 'Alphonse Karr'	30 feet	Culms 1 inch in diameter. Grows densely in slowly expanding clump. Yellow culms, striped green with pink around the nodes, especially when the culm is young. Branches low on the culm. Leaves are grouped In fans.
Bambusa multiplex 'Silver Stripe'	40 feet	White variegated green form. Leaves, culms, and culm sheaths are all green with white striping.
Chusquaea coronalis	15 feet	Central American variety. Whorls of tiny, thin, delicate leaves about ¼ inch wide. Its thin culms arch. Most graceful if kept thinned. *Damaged if below 28°F.*
Chusquaea nigricans	10 feet	Upright, slender black culms with persistent white culm sheaths, which provide checkered effect. Tightly clumping. Narrow leaves.
Chusquaea pitteri	50 feet	A tree climber. Long, arching culms that tangle themselves into tree branches. Roots around the nodes help them stick. Whorls of delicate textured foliage and long side branches that help hold it in a tree. "Looks jungly."
Drepanostachyum falcatum	15 feet	Blue bamboo, Himalayan Mountain bamboo. White powder on its culms makes them appear blue. Purple at the nodes, especially low on the plant. Arches strongly. Variable. Marcia is growing four varieties to study them at maturity. 'Teague's Blue' is extremely vigorous and appears aqua with purple at the base and nodes.
Drepanostachyum hookerianum	15 feet	Striped Himalayan Mountain bamboo. Yellow, green, and pink stripes on the culms. Luxuriant foliage. When the sun hits the culms, they appear raspberry-magenta to purple.
Fargesia nitida	10 feet	Fountain bamboo. Forms a tight clump of thin, purplish gray culms in the shade. Narrow, 2-inch-long leaves.
Otatea aztecorum	20 feet	Mexican weeping bamboo. Forms tight clump of sheathed culms that bend outward under the load of the foliage, which increases yearly. Long, narrow leaves hang down. Marcia thins the clump out yearly.
Pleioblastus akebono	2 feet	A runner. Good ground cover, spreading. White variegation that "looks airbrushed" on a green background.
Pleioblastus viridistriatus chrysophyllus	2½ feet	Another runner. Beware, but so valuable, Marcia says, that it must be mentioned. The foliage is "screaming chartreuse" in spring and has such soft hairs that she calls it "the petting bamboo." May be rampant in a wet climate.

Blue Bamboo
(*Drepanostachyum falcatum*)

ruin." Marcia stops and notes that "they need a little rediscovering," as they are almost completely smothered by the foliage of an orange-flowering abutilon and a trevesia (*T. palmata*). Out with the clippers, and an archaeological exploration begins.

The long, narrow leaves of a "splendid" Australian grass tree (*Xanthorrhoea* sp.) sticks out into the path. Their ends are so soft they tickle as one brushes by them. The path becomes the Path of RIGHTEOUSNESS, each letter embedded into a paving stone. The letters were formed of horseshoes and railroad spikes laid directly on the ground. Thick concrete was patted over them in the shape of stepping-stones. When dry, the paving stones were flipped over and laid in place. Not too many gardens have paths of righteousness, Marcia admits, "And more's the pity."

A garden lavishly planted takes constant care. From the beginning Marcia amended her heavy adobe clay—"when it dries it splits into deep cracks"—with compost, manure, and other organic "odds and ends" by the truckload. It all had to be transported to the backyard by wheelbarrow. Marcia makes her own compost, as well, and tries to give each area a couple of inches each year. She says that the amount of water she uses—very cautiously—is no more than if her garden were a lawn of comparable size. As an economy measure, she siphons bath-

LEFT: **Stationed throughout the garden are playful creatures cut from steel and aged to a warm rusted patina by Marcia's companion, sculptor Mark Bulwinkle. Many are positioned on tall rods to cast dancing shadows across the paths.** BELOW: **An apple tree appears to produce strange fruit, like teapots, teacups, or apples attached to flea market plates—"Plate Flowers" in Marcia's unique garden vocabulary.**

water out of the tub in the house, through the window with a hose, into the garden. She fertilizes very little beyond the compost additions, and she does not encourage rapid growth, believing "lean and mean is better." Judicious, even ferocious, pruning keeps aggressive plants from strangling their less robust neighbors. Sometimes she clears out whole sections. "I go around murdering friends, and I feel bad about it for about a half hour. Then I'm off on the hunt for the new."

ON THE WILD SIDE
Astonishing Plants

MARCIA SAYS she loves plants that "go to extremes. They shock me out of a ho-hum way of seeing and into a reawakening of wonder and pleasure." She is also attracted to surprise in scale, especially gigantism, odd or "stinky fragrance," foliage in colors other than Kelly green, thorns in unexpected sizes or places, relics of ancient times, preposterous shapes, veins, and mottling. "The plants listed below are those that do not fail to astonish me."

PLANT NAME	DESCRIPTION
Aloe ferox	Succulent. Bluish gray-green, 1½-foot leaves spiked over their entire surface with reddish thorns. Trunk will grow to 5 feet. Red-orange flowers in winter. "It stands guard at the curb looking fierce."
Amorphophallus rivieri	Aroid with a 2½-foot leaf, shaped like a snowflake. Snakeskin-patterned stem. Famous flower, which is enormous and fetid. Has not yet bloomed in Marcia's garden.
Arisaema taiwanense	Aroid, 2½-foot-tall jack-in-the-pulpit. Three different patterns, like snakeskin, on its stem. An umbrella of leaves on the top. Both leaves and flower spathe end in an attenuated string.
Aristolochia californica	Rambling 12-foot vine. Blooms in winter with a small greenish pouch-like flower. It is food for the larvae of the black pipevine swallowtail butterfly.
Aristolochia fimbriata	Scandent vine with branches 3 feet long. Rounded, heart-shaped leaves, mottled with white. Small pouch-like flowers, distinguished by their fringe of brown "eyelashes."
Aristolochia gigantea	Climbs to 25 feet. Has 4-inch heart-shaped leaves. In summer it dangles 5-inch-wide velvety maroon, intricately calico-patterned flowers. They narrow into a yellow funnel, leading to a pale green pouch at the back. "They look more like the internal organ of an animal, than a flower."
Begonia 'Little Brother Montgomery'	A 3-by-3-foot pile of pointy leaves, very dark green and maroon with glints of silver. "When it is backlit, it has blood-red gleaming spots. Looks rather sinister for a begonia."
Begonia luxurians	Palm-leaf begonia. Succulent stems with swollen red joints. Umbrellas of 4-inch leaflets.
Begonia 'Paul Hernandez'	Grows to 7 feet. Typical white begonia blossoms. "It satisfies my need for surprise in scale."
Brahea armata	Mexican blue fan palm. Very pale silvery pleated-fan leaves, 4 feet wide. Trunk grows slowly to 40 feet. "Fan palms have an emphatic, graphic exuberance, like comic-book punctuation."

FROM LEFT: *Begonia* 'Little Brother Montgomery' and *Justicia brandegeana*. OPPOSITE: *Aloe ferox*.

Cannamois virgata	Thick red and tan banded shoots mature to bear long brooms of drooping thread-like foliage.
Cyathea medullaris	Black tree fern with 10-foot-long leaves. Leaf petioles and trunk are black and hairy. "You feel tiny standing under it, facing its gorilla fur."
Elegia capensis	South African restios. Whorls of thread-like foliage at intervals up its 5- to 8-foot stems. Stems are topped with dark brown seed heads. Shiny, persistent brown bracts clasp its stems.
Equisetum hyemale	Horsetail, 4 feet tall. Hollow, jointed stems banded in black and white.
Ginkgo biloba	Maidenhair tree. Fan-shaped leaves turn golden yellow in the fall. Pendulous catkin-like flowers borne in clusters. To 25 feet.
Justicia brandegeana	Small flowers protrude from 3-inch-long brick-red bracts, which look like shrimp. Chartreuse-bracted form is 'Shrimps in lime.' "The shrimp plant is always in bloom."
Philodendron selloum	Aroid. Elaborately ruffled and lobed leaves. Improbably huge. Looks tropical and is tender.
Phormium 'Dark Delight'	New Zealand flax. Dark eggplant-purple leaves, 5 feet long, 2 inches wide, without stripes, curve and droop on their ends.
Phormium 'Maori Maiden', 'Rainbow Hybrids'	New Zealand flax. Exciting variations on the pink-yellowish-khaki stripes
Pseudolarix amabilis	Conifer. Deciduous. Soft celadon needles emerge in spring, "looking like tight little brushes that elongate into elegant 1-inch fans." Golden in fall.
Sequoiadendron giganteum pendulum	Conifer. Mutant, weeping redwood. "Narrow, shaggy beast, 15 feet tall, that appears to be lurching along, because of its tilt and undulations."

POT OF GOLD

William J. Radler
Milwaukee, Wisconsin

FROM THE TIME William Radler was a six-year-old boy reading Jackson & Perkins catalogs at his grandparents' home on Sunday afternoons, he has dreamed of roses. When he was nine, he spent his allowance to purchase his first rose. It cost 79 cents. That rose thrived, and by the time Bill was sixteen a hundred roses were growing in his family's backyard.

Forty years later Bill is an award winner. His lifelong passion for roses—and for breeding new varieties—has resulted in his introduction of 'Knock Out', an All-American Rose Selection for the year 2000. Some 250,000 clones of Bill's spectacular new rose will travel the world, ending up in gardens across America and as far away as Europe, South America, Japan, Russia, and New Zealand.

'Knock Out', a disease-resistant, winter-hardy, cerise land-

William J. Radler

"There isn't one perfect rose, but so many that approach perfection."

scape rose, has grabbed the public's attention in part because it was developed in an amateur's backyard, not in a large commercial nursery. The new purple foliage is a foil for the prolific, repeat-flowering bright pink bloom, and the subtle fragrance and compact habit add up to make this a maintenance-free modern garden rose. "It's a little like winning an Oscar," Bill confides. A modest, gentle man, he seems embarrassed by his new fame. "It's pretty heady stuff. But having experienced this pleasure, I want to do it again and again." And so he has: a soft, nonfading, heat-tolerant yellow shrub rose called 'Carefree Sunrise', released in 2001. Several climbers, particularly a brilliant red 'Queen of Hearts' and a yet unnamed delicate pink and salmon that opens to white, are scheduled to follow.

Breeding roses is a long, tedious process; it was fifteen years from the time Bill made the first cross, to 'Knock Out's release on the market. "But the effort is fascinating every step of the way, even though I sometimes think of myself as an indentured servant."

Behind a house he purchased in 1992, some 1,400 roses—all being tested, selected, bred, or monitored—are systematically laid out in beds that mimic the shape of a rainbow. Bill, who has a degree in landscape architecture from the University of Wisconsin at Madison, designed the beds, which total more than 800 running feet. Their arched configuration covers three-quarters of an acre. "It seemed more aesthetically interesting than straight beds, and it's just as practical," he notes. When the roses are in full bloom in mid-June, the effect is that of the sun shining through a thousand prisms, exploding in shades of pink, lavender, red, orange, and yellow.

Bill started breeding in his spare time during his twenty-year tenure as the director of the Boerner Botanical Gardens and Arboretum in Milwaukee. Discouraged by the winter dieback on his own roses, he nonetheless believed that there was no reason why roses could not be hardy in his Zone 4 climate. As modern roses were increasingly bred for color, flower size, and fragrance, the features of winter hardiness and disease resistance had fallen by the wayside. Granted, Bill says, it is ideal to have little winter dieback so that the gardener can determine how to prune and shape his roses, but Bill will settle for crown hardiness. (Since he prunes his roses back in the spring anyway, he says, "Who cares if you are pruning back live or dead material?") He seeks roses that will survive without the

PREVIOUS PAGES: **The eleven rainbow-shaped beds where Bill Radler subjects his roses to rigorous testing cover a quarter of an acre. A 300-foot path bisects the beds and runs from the terrace to a compost area in the woods.** THIS PAGE, OPPOSITE: **To breed 'Knock Out', an All-American Rose Selection for 2000, Bill used eight different roses, including his own hybrids and commercially available tea, floribunda, and shrub roses.** ABOVE LEFT: **One of Bill's hybrid roses, 'Queen of Hearts', a red climber.** ABOVE: **'Carefree Sunshine', a non-fading yellow shrub rose, another of Bill's hybrids.**

BELOW, RIGHT: **From Bill's office window, where he keeps track of his roses on a computer, he can survey his entire nursery and his terrace garden.** BELOW: **'Lilian Austin', named for David Austin's mother and introduced in 1973, is one of Austin's most beautiful**

labor-intensive wrapping and bundling for winter protection, a process that, even when followed, is far from foolproof. "In this garden it is survival of the fittest," he declares.

Bill began to breed for hardiness but soon set his sights higher. "Why not disease resistance, as well?" he asked. "Repeat flowering? Self-cleaning? Compact habit? Fragrance? Fall color? Thornlessness? Nonsuckering? Weather-tolerant blooms that can take anything Mother Nature delivers, like wind and rain or scorching heat? Long-lasting bloom both in the garden and as cut flowers?" It soon became clear that his aim was nothing less than the perfect rose.

It takes generations of mixing and matching roses with coveted attributes to hatch a win-

English Roses. Its flowers are large and full-petaled, growing on a compact bush with glossy green foliage. Bill keeps it in his own garden to use as a parent in his breeding program—and recommends it to other rose aficionados.

ner. Negating a rose's weak features is as big a part of the process as emphasizing the strong. Bill began to collect named and patented roses with some of the characteristics he sought, and by marrying one to another he strove for strong genes of sterling quality. It is a painstaking but surprisingly low-tech process.

Bill holds up his forefinger, demonstrating that "everybody has the right tool to make a cross. We must be the bee." First he selects two roses and removes their petals. He clips the anthers of the male rose with tiny scissors and drops them into a clean porcelain jar; as the anthers dry, the pollen—a fine golden dust—separates from them. Bill then clips off the anthers of the recipient rose so that none of its own pollen remains and the pistil, a miniature cauliflower-like mound, is revealed in the middle of the blossom. Bill rubs his forefinger across the harvested pollen dust, collecting it on the end of his finger, then taps the pollen onto the pistil.

To prevent further pollination by either insect or wind, which would render his cross impure, Bill wraps "the future hip" in a tube of aluminum foil labeled with the name of the female parent (the first name listed) and that of the male parent. The foil is not fastened too tightly, as the rose needs to continue to receive nutrients through its stem in order to produce a seed-filled hip. If the cross fails—that is, if the pistil is not pollinated—the stem and head fall to the ground.

The foil-wrapped future hip remains on the shrub as it matures throughout the summer. In the fall, "if we're lucky," Bill opens the foil and finds a perfectly ripe red, orange, or golden hip. He harvests those hips and places them in labeled plastic bags. While Bill has one dedicated assistant, Kathi Beilfuss, preparing the seeds for germination is a laborious effort, and the hips are often stored for periods of time before they are readied for the process.

ROSES ON THE MARKET
Bill Radler's Recommendations

BILL RADLER grows his competitors' roses just to see how they measure up to his standards. "Most don't," he admits. However, when a commercially grown rose has a quality he admires, he may incorporate it into his breeding. "We might as well use each other's work as stepping-stones; there's no point in going backwards."

NAME	DESCRIPTION
Rosa 'Abraham Darby'	Peach; old-fashioned form; fragrant
Rosa 'Aloha'	Pink; old-fashioned form; fragrant
Rosa 'Appleblossom'	Light pink; cluster-flowered
Rosa 'Ambridge Rose'	Pastel orange; old-fashioned form; fragrant
Rosa 'Amiga Mia'	Pink
Rosa 'Country Dancer'	Pink
Rosa 'Countryman'	Large; deep pink
Rosa 'First Light'	Pale pink with maroon stamens; 5-petaled
Rosa 'Flower Carpet'	Glowing pink clusters
Rosa 'Folksinger'	Palest orange
Rosa 'Frederick Mistral'	Double pink, fragrant
Rosa 'Frontier Twirl'	Large, deep coral

NAME	DESCRIPTION
Rosa 'Les Sjulin'	Large, pink bicolor
Rosa 'Lilian Austin'	Large, pink bicolor, fragrant
Rosa 'Maleguena'	Pink
Rosa 'Nearly Wild'	Light pink, 5 petals
Rosa 'Paloma Blanca'	White
Rosa 'Perdida'	Pale orange, old-fashioned form; fragrant
Rosa 'Perlie Mae'	Palest peach blend
Rosa 'Prairie Harvest'	Palest yellow; fragrant
Rosa 'Serendipity'	Palest orange
Rosa 'Summer Wind'	Pale salmon-pink, 5 petals
Rosa 'The Fairy'	Small; pale pink in large clusters
Rosa 'Wanderin' Wind'	Light pink, fragrant
Rosa 'William Baffin'	Climber, deep pink

THE RADLER SYSTEM
Transplanting Rose Seedlings

Seedlings should be transplanted from plastic bags to pots only after cotyledons have fully emerged from the seed.

1. With a heated fork, melt a 1¼-inch slit across the bottom of a 6.4-ounce Styrofoam cup.

2. Fill the cup halfway with coarse horticultural-grade perlite. Sprinkle one-quarter teaspoon of 10-20-5 time-release (3 to 4 months) fertilizer, like Osmacote, over the perlite. Place a slanted layer of cat litter (calcine clay) mixed 1:1 with Redi-Erth over the perlite.

3. Gently pick up the seedling with a bamboo skewer. Place it on the slanted layer with the root on the lowest side. Sprinkle more calcine clay to cover just the root of the seedling.

4. Mix a solution of 1 teaspoon 15-30-15 water-soluble concentrated fertilizer designated for acid soil–loving plants to 1 gallon of water. Water the seedling well. Cover the pot with a clear plastic shot glass.

5. Place the pot under cool white fluorescent lights at a distance of approximately 1 to 2 inches. If possible, keep the environment at 55–65°F, although room temperature will also work.

6. Place the planted cups in a tray of water. Keep the trays filled with ⅛ to ½ inch of water at all times.

7. After the seedlings have developed two full sets of leaves, remove the shot glasses. Feed the seedlings weekly by pouring 1 quart of the same 15-30-15 fertilizer solution into each 12-by-24-inch tray.

8. Take the plants outside only after the danger of frost is over, and harden them off in a protected spot for at least a week before planting them in the ground.

CLOCKWISE FROM TOP LEFT: **A tough, winter-hardy climbing rose with pastel pink blooms and a honeyed fragrance; this rose in the early stages of testing has pale orange to pink blooms and gives off an old-rose fragrance; rosy pink old-fashioned form and chartreuse foliage; Bill's yellow mutation of 'Autumn Sunset' occurred spontaneously and exhibits fine winter hardiness and blackspot-disease resistance.**

The hips are peeled open, and inside are future rose plants—seeds that can number from two to fifty. Bill carefully lays the seeds on pads of wet paper towels, then labels them, bags them, and places them in the refrigerator, where temperatures under 40°F break down the chemicals that prevent germination. Three to six weeks after germination, which takes from six to eighteen weeks, the cotyledons, or seed leaves, emerge and the seedlings are ready to be planted.

These days Bill starts the winter season with a thousand seedlings, which he weeds down to five hundred over the next several months. The seedlings are lined in a nursery-like environment. Cool white fluorescent lights on chains hanging as close to the plants as possible glow around the clock.

Six-ounce Styrofoam cups, slashed across the bottom with a reciprocating saw to ensure drainage, house the seedlings; they are set in flat trays of water so the plants can wick up the water as they need it. "The key is to prevent the seedlings from drying out," says Bill. "And that one trick has multiplied their growth by a factor of three." Since he uses no insecticide or fungicide—either in the basement or outside—he must be vigilant. Creatures like mealy bugs or spider mites can charge like an army. Bill's favorite spray solution is a mixture of 1 tablespoon corn oil and 1 tablespoon dishwashing detergent to a gallon of water. "It even kills their eggs," he notes gleefully.

In spring, Bill must make room in the already filled beds of what he calls his laboratory. He tags bad performers and frequently pitches them out. Editing is ruthless. "I dispose of five hundred rose plants a year. Breeding is unpredictable. Most of the time you get the worst of the parents. If you're very, very lucky your success rate might be 1 percent." Meanwhile the babies, still in their pots but now old enough to face the real world, are hardened-off in a protected fenced playpen next to the house for at least a week before being transplanted in the beds.

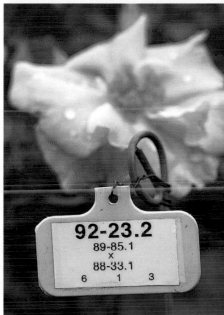

An automatic overhead watering system provides the roses with about an inch of water a week, which has made an impressive difference in the plants' growth. Rejecting the commonly accepted practice of drip irrigation, he says, "I am actually trying to encourage diseases." Only through studying problem roses can he come up with a cause or a cure.

A mental map— Bill has a photographic memory—takes him on a regular route of travel through the garden. A rose with promise commands his attention; like a prize stud or brood mare, its characteristics are faithfully recorded. When a rose passes Bill's muster, he sends it—cuttings or scion wood in the form of bud eyes, wrapped in wet newspaper for the trip—to commercial growers for further testing. In 2000 he sent out ten different varieties. After further testing by commercial growers, some roses are submitted for competition in the All-American Rose Selection, a trial program conducted at twenty-two official test gardens across the country. Up to 50 winners each year are virtually assured of heading for the general market, though the growers make the final decision as to a rose's marketability. Nursery stock must then be built up, a process that takes a good five years. The registration of the new rose's name occurs with the International Registration Authority for Roses, which is under the aegis of the American Rose Society. With 'Knock Out's commercial debut, Bill is now considered a pro. "I lose my amateur status with the first royalty check," he says.

Bill observes that man has had a love affair with the rose for centuries, and many have accepted the challenge to breed new varieties. "My goal is to give gardeners the roses of their dreams without all the headaches."

TOP: A particularly lovely soft peach climbing rose, which grows on the front of Bill's house, has been crossed with several possible mates. For the summer months, it wears a half dozen aluminum tubes over its future hips. ABOVE: Every rose in Bill's garden bears an identifying number, according to botanical gardens' standard system of acquisition: the year, the lot, and the number. The top number indicates the year the rose was crossed; the smaller numbers are those of the rose's parents.

STONE AGE

Sarah Draney
Marbletown, New York

IN A FIELD fringed by a new-growth woodland a spare, modest house stands in a stark clearing. There is no lawn; instead, surrounding the building is an astonishing garden that features piles of rock, the bleached trunks of dead trees that point to the sky, rusted iron teepees, and other shards of civilization. These vignettes, which are hauntingly familiar and strangely beautiful, are not the remains of a prehistoric society, but the work of a bold contemporary imagination.

"I started to make a little garden out in front of the house, and I just kept going," recalls Sarah Draney, painter, sculptor, and "stoney." "I thought I'd come here and spend most of my time in my studio. But my garden and my work have become one. I never planned to make such a garden," she muses as she looks across the

Sarah Draney

"I think of stones as the garden's carpet, out of which all things grow."

sculpture garden that seems more fictional moonscape than upstate New York farmland. "It just happened. I've always been an artist; I never intended to be a gardener."

Sarah walks the paths she has cut through her woods, hauling dead cedar trees or rocks covered with lichen back to the garden. Local antique shops yield architectural remnants: a finial from a marble column, a carved detail from a lintel, a fragment of a millstone; and Sarah frequents the dump to salvage the rusted iron remains of a potbellied stove, a farmer's bed, or a child's school desk. The shapes of these carefully chosen pieces—organic circles and ovals or geometric squares and hexagons—are her inspiration and her raw material. "I am attracted to things that appear to be in the process of disappearing," she explains.

A ceramist for decades, she has always been partial to plant forms and primitive domestic configurations. Now she creates pieces to be combined with found objects as elements of assemblages in her garden. Ladders, sticks tied with cord, or wire joined with knots of clay lean against piles of rock. Tiny ceramic houses raised on stilts are placed in circles of smooth pebbles. Objects, at once abstract and referential, defy the rules of scale and confuse the eye.

PREVIOUS PAGES AND THIS PAGE, BELOW AND LEFT: **Sarah Draney's assemblages, formerly the domain of studio and gallery, are now created in situ. These "combines" are the bones of a garden that changes dramatically from season to season. In the winter the garden is sparc, eerie, even desolate, and in summer, lush, abundant, and almost impenetrable. "My work is part of a continuum growing out of nature—**

They suggest ceremony or ritual, but there is no text to inform. "I've never been comfortable attaching words to things," says Sarah. "Once words are put with an object, they seem so permanent. I don't want to define specifically."

Sarah was raised in a family of gardeners in Hyde Park, New York, and realizes that she learned more than she thought about cultivating the earth when she was very young. But as she grew up, she gave more thought to becoming an artist than a gardener. She attended Bard College, close to her Hudson Valley home, and later transferred to the San Francisco Art

briefly present it will disappear back into the earth," Sarah says. OPPOSITE: *Sedum spectabile* 'Stardust' and *Portulaca grandiflora,* **planted in pots, are nestled among the found ornaments in Sarah's garden.**

BELOW: **Another area of the garden seen in dead of winter and full summer.**
OPPOSITE: **In creating vignettes, Sarah says she considers color, weight,**

Institute, where she enjoyed the 1960s freethinking atmosphere. There she realized that art could be made from *any* material and placed in *any* environment. She moved back to New York City and has maintained a studio there for twenty-five years.

In 1992, Sarah and her husband, Herman Greitzer, a retired lawyer and art collector, decided they needed a country retreat. Sarah wanted land, "something that felt hidden," and

texture, shape, perspective, space, light, and a sense of movement. "To some extent I'm in control, but the constant changing of the natural world is out of my control, and that's what is both exciting and curious to me: the unexpected versus the expected."

Herman needed a vista. They bought 8½ acres of farmland an hour and a half north of New York City. A barn covered in faded yellow tarpaper, a remnant from the property's former life as a chicken farm, announces the entrance to the property, where a dirt road sweeps around its wide girth.

The spare house, open and inviting, features 10-foot windows that face a gentle landscape of fields and rolling hills. Stained gray, the exterior seems to reflect the varying shades of the stone that surrounds it. When Sarah decided to make her first garden, she instinctively began to work with stone, and it has remained her material of choice.

"There are parallels between the landscape here and in Ireland," Sarah observes. "It seems

SET IN STONE
Plants for a Gravel Garden

BOTANICAL NAME	COMMON NAME	DESCRIPTION
Achillea 'Coronation Gold'	Yarrow	Clump forming; silvery gray leaves; yellow flat flower heads; 3 feet
Achillea millefolium	Wild yarrow	Mat-forming clumps; midgreen leaves; creamy white flowers; 3 feet
Achillea 'Moonshine'		Clump-forming; delicate gray-green leaves; light yellow daisy-like flower heads; 2 feet
Agastache foeniculum	Anise hyssop	Gray-green leaves; spikes of mauve flowers; 3 to 5 feet; reseeds among the stones
Alcea rosea 'Nigra'	Black hollyhock	Vigorous, upright; rounded, hairy light green leaves; chocolate-maroon flowers with yellow throats; 6 feet
Artemisia abrotanum	Southernwood	Shrub; aromatic gray-green leaves; yellowish flower heads; to 3 feet
Artemisia ludoviciana var. *albula* 'Silver King'	Western mugwort	Compact; clump-forming; lance-shaped silver leaves; 30 inches
Artemisia ludoviciana var. *albula* 'Silver Queen'	Western mugwort	Compact, clump-forming; large silver leaves; 30 inches
Artemisia schmidtiana	Silvermound	Low, tufted, forming a silver carpet of silky-hairy leaves; yellow flower heads; 12 inches
Artemisia stellerana		Compact, prostrate; deeply toothed, hairy gray foliage; 8 inches
Calluna vulgaris 'Elsie Frye'	Scotch heather	Rounded, mat-forming, evergreen shrub; dark green leaves; yellow flowers; 10 inches
Chasmanthium latifolium	Northern sea oats	Clumping grass; drooping bamboo-like foliage; turns copper in fall; 3 feet
Comptonia peregrina	Sweet fern	Suckering shrub with feathery fern-like leaves; very sweet smell in hot weather; 2 to 3 feet
Cynara cardunculus	Cardoon	Clump-forming; spiny, silvery gray leaves; purple flower heads; 5 feet
Delosperma sphalmanthoides		Tight mat forming like a pincushion; prostrate branches with tiny finger-like leaves, magenta flowers; 2 inches
Digitalis lanata	Foxglove	Clump-forming; oblong lance-shaped midgreen leaves; dense racemes of pale cream flowers; 2 feet
Echinops ritro 'Veitch's Blue'	Globe thistle	Compact, clump-forming; stiff, spiny gray leaves; ball-shaped flowers of dark blue; 3 feet
Euphorbia dulcis 'Chameleon'		Rhizomatous; erect stems with lance-shaped rich purple leaves; purple-tinged yellow green flowers; 16 inches
Euphorbia polychroma	Cushion spurge	Clump-forming; oblong, dark green leaves; yellowish green flowers; 2 feet
Lavandula angustifolia	Lavender	Compact, bushy; gray-green leaves; pale to deep purple flowers in dense spikes; to 3 feet
Lavandula angustifolia 'Hidcote'	Lavender	Compact, bushy; silvery green leaves; dark purple flowers; to 2 feet
Lavandula angustifolia 'Nana Alba'	White lavender	Very compact, bushy; spikes of white flowers; 12 inches
Miscanthus sinensis 'Cabaret'	Japanese silver grass	White, linear stripe up center of leaves; 6 feet tall

Miscanthus sinensis 'Morning Light'	Japanese silver grass	White stripe on leaf margins; 5 to 6 feet tall
Miscanthus sinensis 'Zebrinus'	Zebra grass	Arching foliage with yellowish white bands across; 5 to 6 feet
Nepeta faassenii	Catmint	Clumping; small gray-green leaves; spikes of lavender flowers; 2 feet
Onoclea sensibilis	Sensitive fern	Upright, arching pale green fronds; emerging fronds may be pinkish bronze in spring; 2 feet
Panicum virgatum 'Heavy Metal'	Switch grass	Upright clumps; stiff, metallic blue foliage; 3 to 3½ feet
Perovskia atriplicifolia	Russian sage	Upright subshrub; silvery gray-green leaves; panicles of tubular, violet-blue flowers; 3 feet
Rosa rugosa **var.** *alba*	Rugosa rose	Dense species rose with prickly stems; wrinkled, leathery, dark green leaves; fragrant white flowers; 6 feet
Ruta graveolens 'Blue Beauty'	Rue	Rounded shrub; blue-green foliage; yellow flowers; self-seeds in stones; 20 inches
Salvia elegans	Pineapple sage	Subshrub; softly hairy, pineapple-scented midgreen leaves; terminal panicles of bright scarlet flowers; treat as an annual; to 6 feet
Salvia officinalis	Common sage	Clump-forming; gray-green woolly, aromatic leaves; spikes of violet flowers; to 3 feet
Salvia officinalis 'Holt's Mammoth'	Sage	Compact form; long, wide gray leaves; 3 feet
Salvia officinalis 'Icterina'	Sage	Compact form; green leaves with wide golden margin; 2 feet
Salvia officinalis 'Purpurascens'	Purple sage	Clump forming; gray-green and purple woolly, aromatic leaves; 12 inches
Sagina subulata	Pearlwort	Mat-forming; pointed, linear green leaves; white flowers; 1 inch
Sagina subulata 'Aurea'	Golden pearlwort	Mat-forming; pointed, linear chartreuse leaves; white flowers; 1 inch
Santolina chamaecyparissus	Lavender cotton	Compact, rounded clump; aromatic, feathery gray-green foliage; yellow flowers; to 20 inches
Sedum 'Herbstfreude'	Sedum 'Autumn Joy'	Clump-forming; bushy; toothed, glaucous dark green-gray leaves; pink flowers, turning bronze, then copper in fall; to 30 inches
Sedum spathulifolium 'Cape Blanco'		Vigorous, mat-forming; innermost leaves heavily powdered with white bloom; white flowers; 4 inches
Sedum spectabile 'Stardust'		Clump-forming upright; slightly scalloped gray-green leaves; silvery pink flowers; 30 inches
Sedum telephium subsp. *atropurpureum*		Clump-forming; very dark purple stems and leaves; pink flowers with red-orange centers; 2 feet
Stachys byzantina 'Silver Carpet'	Lamb's ears	Clump-forming; lance-shaped, silvery gray leaves; nonflowering; to 12 inches
Thymus × *citriodorus*	Lemon thyme	Bushy, rounded mat; lemon fragrant fine midgreen foliage; 12 inches; spreads around stones
Thymus pseudolanuginosus	Woolly thyme	Prostrate shrublet; tiny, elliptic gray-green foliage; pale pink flowers; 3 inches
Thymus vulgaris	Common thyme	Cushion-forming mat; fine, aromatic gray-green foliage; pale purple flowers; 6 to 12 inches; spreads around stones
Verbascum 'Southern Charm'	Mullen	Basil rosette; gray foliage; rose, lilac, and apricot flowers; 3 feet
Verbascum phoeniceum	Purple mullen	Wrinkled, veined dark green foliage; violet to purple flowers; to 4 feet
Verbascum thapsus	Wild mullen	Basil rosette; gray foliage; yellow flowers, allowed to remain through winter; birds eat the seeds; 3 to 6 feet
Yucca flaccida 'Ivory Tower'	Yucca	Basil rosettes of dark blue-green; lance-shaped leaves; to 2 feet; green-tinged, creamy-white flowers on spikes to 5 feet

BELOW: **Since Sarah finds inspiration for her ceramic sculptures, like the Tower, in natural forms, when placed**

out in nature the finished objects create an ambiguous tension between what she has made and what she has found. The colors for her ceramic glazes also reiterate those she sees in nature or on artifacts in stages of rust or decay, suggesting their "return to the earth." OPPOSITE: **A chair form placed in a bed of creeping thyme is intended to nudge perceptions of time and reality.**

so pared down, and the bare bones show—the wild things and all that stone. Plants love the protective crevices created by quantities of rock. And Irish gardens are often deeply mysterious. The people are superstitious and respectful of the ancient world. If there is a mound in the landscape, a stone monolith, or an old tree, farmers don't touch it. They farm around it."

Early on, Sarah visited a local quarry and selected large flat stones to make the base of the first garden, a half-circle in front of the house. She discovered that she lived in an area of old quarries, from which, historically, the stone was transported by barge down the Hudson River to New York City. She befriended the quarry owners and encouraged them to find her unusual forms. "These men have responded to my enthusiasm," she reports, observing that when they deliver stone they are anxious to please her in placing the rock. "They seem delighted to move a stone even a couple of inches." And, Sarah regularly orders stone by the truckload. "I keep adding and adding," she says.

Boulders, miniature mountain ranges, are positioned to provide height and, like Chinese scholars' rocks, to serve as tantalizing forms for contemplation. "My largest rock, which weighs about 3 tons, was chosen for its white quartzy, limestone-like surface," she notes. "I also love cement, because it looks like stone." She finds aged planters and drainpipes, often broken. Sarah also rescued some 4-foot-square highway drains that had been dumped by the highway department at the back of a quarry. They are like giant troughs in which Sarah has planted a collection of sedums. Grinding stones, in a range of sizes and conditions, are set in the ground; they, too, hold sedums as well as hens and chickens.

Nothing is static in the garden. Sarah rearranges constantly, like a designer trying furniture in different locations in a house; she is looking for fresh solutions, provocative ideas for making a garden. By falling for stone, originally an aesthetic, rather than a horticultural, decision, Sarah inadvertently created unique growing conditions: a dry microclimate with excellent drainage that pushes her Zone 5 envelope, as stone holds the warmth of the sun. "I know I'm not supposed to be able to grow Corsican mint, but it thrives here."

Gravel, or peastone, which in Sarah's area is prehistoric riverbed stone, is her mulch. "I can't think of any plant that does not like gravel—even roses. I seem to have less disease and fewer bugs on my roses than other gardeners because of the gravel." However, she cautions that even plants that are reputed to be drought-resistant need some coddling and watering during their first season. Once they have become acclimated to the dry conditions, they are self-sufficient. Summer drought, which can reduce other gardeners to hand wringing and rain dancing, doesn't ruffle Sarah's equilibrium.

Using gravel as her mulch has not made the garden any easier to maintain, however. "It is very labor-intensive," Sarah maintains. "Whatever falls to the ground must be removed, or I'll have muck in which weeds will quickly grow. Cleaning it up each spring is always a

Sarah leaves most of her plants standing through the winter, which helps define the garden's character. The

tremendous job, one that is ongoing until August, when the growing comes to a halt."

In selecting her plant palette, Sarah studied what grew close by, outside the confines of the garden. She selected wild things—"big guys," like poke, mullen, thistle, sweet fern, and even wild grape—from her fields and invited them to inhabit the garden, though with serious

added benefit is the aviary-like atmosphere created by the presence of seed heads, particularly those of the statuesque plants and a range of grasses, like the miscanthus (*M. 'Pupurascens', M. sinensis 'Zebrinus',* and *M. sinensis 'Morning Light'*) and sea oats (*Uniola paniculata*). All provide winter food for the birds.

policing. Poke (*Phytolacca americana*), which can reach 10 feet, can be a pest, and she is careful not to let it go to seed. "I love things that soar upward, but if you allow one to grow, you can end up with a million."

While Sarah leans toward native plants, she cannot resist exotics that are large of leaf and generous of stature. "I love the castor bean plant—*Ricinus communis, R. c.* 'Carmencita' with bronze-red foliage and *R. c.* 'Gibsonii', with its deeply forked and glossy leaves or the dark maroon *Angelica gigas,* a magnificent specimen." Sarah also concentrates on Mediterranean plants and those with gray foliage; they prosper in the garden's dry, rocky conditions. "Lavender, while trickier to grow than the natives, is worth the effort. I keep the peastone up to its crown, and it likes those conditions." Lamb's ears, salvia, thyme, and santolina form clumps at the path's edges.

When Sarah wants to introduce a new plant into her garden, she buys at least three of them, planting each in a different location in her garden to ascertain where the plant will thrive. Often, she says, she loses one or two, but the last one will tell her where that variety will be happiest. Then she adds more to create a grouping. "I've always made groups of pieces

in my work, and I've just carried that preference over into my gardening," she notes.

Her partiality for multiples extends to outbuildings as well. To store wood for the stove, ceramics that need winter protection, and a myriad of garden tools, Sarah has built a series of sheds in the garden. She likes the idea that they make a cluster of barn buildings, like those that were erected, from necessity, on old farms. "Often sheds were cobbled together from leftover things, making them look like a quilt or a collage."

When terracing the sloped hillside that has made her first garden, Sarah immediately visualized the space as a stage. In retrospect, she muses, "Having a garden is like producing an ongoing show for yourself. It's a huge exhibition, moving and changing all the time. My next fantasy is to order a pair of industrial concrete staircases and set them out in the landscape, paint them with milk so the moss grows, and then just go and sit on them."

THE BOLD ONE

Linda J. Cochran
Bainbridge Island, Washington

"IF YOU ARE LOOKING for subtle," says Linda Cochran, "don't look here." No alpine miniatures or woodland wildflowers enter this gardener's vocabulary. Rather, Linda takes her inspiration from the tropics, the jungles, the mountains of the Himalayas, the homes of bold, colorful plant giants.

A rare rice paper plant (*Tetrapanax papyriferus*) and an exotic *Paulownia tomentosa* stand taller than Linda—by twice her height or more. Fantastic foliage follows suit: the foliage of the umbrella-like *Astilboïdes tabularis* and the glossy, deeply lobed *Potophylum peltatum* stretch at least two feet across, outclassed only by *Gunnera tinctoria* with its colossal 5-foot leaves.

Textural surprises, like the pleated fans of a palm (*Trachycarpus fortunei*) or a silvery *Melianthus major* contrast with the elongated,

Linda J Cox

"I make a master plan for the shapes of beds, but plant combinations are more spontaneous; they begin with just a flash of an idea."

PREVIOUS PAGES, LEFT: **In Linda Cochran's terrace garden, a stylized** *Meconopsis* **poppy fountain sculpture by innovative Bainbridge artists Little and Lewis sets the tone for drama. Staged around the pool are** *Bougainvilla* **'Raspberry Ice',** *Verbena*

'Homestead Purple', *Pennisetum orientale* **'Tall Tails', and** *Verbena bonariensis.* TOP RIGHT: **The entrance gate opens to an oval lawn surrounded by a daringly conceived border that contrasts texture, scale, and color. It includes Young's weeping birch,** *Carex elata* **'Bowles' Golden',** *Ligularia dentata* **'Othello', and** *Euphorbia wallichii.* THIS PAGE, ABOVE: **The soft gray-green foliage of** *Melianthus major* **contrasts with the upright spikes of** *Canna* **'Tropicana' and the arching** *Phygelius* **'African Queen'.**

pointed swords of a cordyline. Reverberating jewel tones—a shocking pink *Canna ehmannii,* a fiery orange *Crocosmia* 'Emily McKenzie', ruby-red *Dahlia* 'Bednall Beauty', magenta bougainvillea called 'Strawberry Ice', and violet *Verbena* 'Homestead Purple'—are echoed in masses throughout the garden. Such compositions are typical of Linda's propensity for the oversize and brilliant plants.

"Views are changing, but traditionally, purists frowned on these 'mad' imports for northwestern gardens," Linda says, laughing. "They thought we should heed the formal features and planting palettes of England, Japan, and Italy for our gardening style. Of course, those concepts were originally imports, too." She continues: "I certainly incorporate ideas from those cultures. But I'm interested in absorbing what the rest of the world—the Southwest, Mexico, South America, Africa, the East—has to offer. The key to this garden is that I seek plants that come from habitats similar to our Zone 8 climate, wherever that may be. I try to grow what is hardy here—and that is a surprising range of plants. This is Canna-Banana Land!"

Linda's father was a missionary, and Linda spent her early childhood in Iraq and Lebanon. She was seven when the family returned to the United States, settling on the coast of southern Oregon, and she calls the Pacific Northwest home. Yet Linda's childhood impressions, particularly of palms and bougainvilleas from Beirut, must have had some effect on her adult vision. Still stronger influences, she says, are painters of Mexico and the Southwest who converse in broad bands of contrasting color. Linda admires Gauguin, as evidenced in her striking combinations of tropical-looking plants. She observes, "Gauguin turned his back on tradition to create an entirely new painting language—in subject matter and in rhythmic patterns of color."

Linda was in her thirties when she started gardening. She knew from the moment she picked up a spade that her métier was nontraditional. "I fell for big foliage, for plants with a powerful presence, and I have never wavered." In 1981 Linda and David Jergus, then partners in a husband-and-wife law firm, moved to Bainbridge Island, a ferry ride across Puget Sound from Seattle, in search of land to fulfill their dreams. The half acre they purchased there soon became too confining. In 1989 a daughter, Jennifer, was born, and Linda retired from the legal practice to devote her energy to raising her daughter and creating a garden.

In 1993 the couple bought a house based on an Arizona plan. "Its open nature suited our lifestyle and fit with what I imagined could be our garden," Linda recalls, emphasizing the importance of integrating house and garden into a unified whole. The architecture dictated a blend of Southwest and Northwest before a handful of earth was turned over.

The house came with 5 acres of gently sloping land that finally allowed Linda's gardening

OPPOSITE: **The front garden includes mass plantings of** *Euphorbiu seguieriana, E. characia* **subsp.** *wulfenii* **'Lambrook Gold',** *Agastache rupestris, Canna* **'Pretoria', and** *Stipa tenuissima.* TOP LEFT: **Draped by "the clash of the titans"—crimson glory vine (***Vitex coignetiae***), which turns brilliant red-orange in the fall, complementing the red foliage and black fruit of** *Parthenocissus tricuspidata* **and a large-leafed golden hops (***Humulus lupus* **'Sunbeam')—the wall enclosing Linda's garden has all but disappeared. "I suppose you could say the wall is English, but the roofed gate is Japanese," observes Linda. A long border is planted with masses of** *Verbena* **'Homestead Purple'.** ABOVE RIGHT: **The focal point of the entrance garden is a 10-foot Egyptian column fountain, created by Little and Lewis and crowned with water forget-me-nots (***Myosotis palustrus***) kept moist by constantly trickling water.**

impulses to take flight. On the quiet street lined with native red cedars, Douglas firs and ferns, a startling 30-by-120-foot mounded bed that runs the length of the house's facade announces Linda's garden. Masses of cannas with leaves of gold and copper, a silver cut-leaf sport of *Cynara cardunculus, Chesquea couleou,* a lacy clump-forming bamboo, orange-red flowering *Kniphofia multiflora,* long flaming blooms of *Salvia involucrata* 'Bethellii', clusters of blue wheat grass (*Elymus magellanicus*), and rust-colored *Carex secta* set the unconventional tone.

Linda recalls that her first priority was to create a master plan. The layout of the garden, for which she had assistance from a local landscape architect, Bart Berg, has changed little. Practical solutions, like proper drainage, as well as aesthetic issues were addressed. Behind the house, where flooding was a constant problem, the grade was raised 1½ feet, which also provided a smoother transition between house and garden. While many of the crisply edged beds are curved in great abstract shapes, the garden is anchored with axial lines. These long, open vistas extend from north to south and east to west.

One of the first areas to take shape was the bog garden. The unsightly 6-foot-deep drainage ditch, lined with black basalt rock, that parallels the front of the property has vanished under a camouflage of herculean plants. Majestic stands of magenta-flowered Joe-Pye weed (*Eupatorium maculatum*) jostle with gunneras, native umbrella-leafed *Darmera peltata,* and oversize marsh spurge *Euphorbia palustrus,* which Linda describes as a looking "like *polychroma* on steroids."

A small oval pond was constructed just above the bog. A 10-foot columnar fountain extends above the surrounding plants. Linda believes the sound of water—she has fountains both in the front and back gardens—is integral to the feeling of separation from the outside world.

With the structure of the garden in place, Linda concentrates on refining her planting compositions. Over the years she has developed her personal design principles "by intuition." Many gardeners weave a ribbon of individual plants through a grouping, she observes; her preference is to plant in broad sweeps, generous numbers of the same plant, from three to more than a dozen large plants in large clumps.

In creating each vignette, Linda combines three kinds of plant forms. First are the broad-

leafed plants, which can be divided into two subcategories: broad-horizontal like persicaria, calocasia, astilboïdes, and hosta and broad-vertical like canna and banana. The second group is linear and includes grasses, iris, crocosmia, daylily, gladiola, and hardy gingers. She calls the third form "busy" or "amorphous." It contains geraniums, euphorbias, thalictrums, and melianthus. "It's a simple idea, but when I'm struggling with an area, if I make a grouping of these three foliage shapes, it generally works," she says.

While Linda's first consideration in a composition is a plant's leaf shape, the color of its foliage is a close second. Here the myriad hues and shades of foliage—green, yellow, purple, gray, and variegated—enter the picture. She used to mix a number of foliage colors in a single composition. Lately she selects an individual plant with a strong foliage color as a centerpiece and builds a grouping around it in quieter shades of green. A plant singled out takes on a more powerful attitude, she believes.

Linda uses many variegated plants—grasses, shrubs, and perennials, particularly those that are edged or striped with yellow—often incorporating more than one variegated plant in a single arrangement. "Of course, purists would say no-no to that. The one rule I do follow is that I do not mix yellow and white variegation in the same group. There is not enough contrast between them."

Linda has developed her own flower color theory. She identifies a trio of color families—oranges to yellows, blues to purples, pinks to reds—and she will blend all three in one

LEFT: **In some of Linda's audacious plant combinations, it is not the flowers, but rather vast swaths of foliage color—like the burgundy and copper of** *Rhododendron bureavii* **hybrids, the golden**

arrangement. However, she will not combine a blue-red with an orange-red in the same grouping. "I don't like white," Linda declares, "and other than the few variegated foliage plants that have white, I do not use white in the garden." Where others add white to brighten up an area, to break a color mass, or intensify a color, Linda uses a soft yellow, which she feels accomplishes the same mission but with heightened results.

Not by plants alone are compositions made. Throughout the garden, Linda accents areas with objects, boldly chosen, and often daringly painted. Glazed pots from Asia are filled with water and covered with velvety azolla and water lettuce. A brilliant blue jar contrasts with a variegated Jacob's ladder (*Polemonium* 'Briese d'Anjou'). The fountain pool on the terrace was constructed with concrete, pigmented with a rosy color, and then painted by Bainbridge

Hakonechloa macra 'Aureola', a deep shiny green *Euphorbia amygdaloides* var. *robbiae*—that seem to erupt from beds and flow out onto the lawns. ABOVE: **A pair of vivid turquoise terra-cotta eggs, set off by the deep greenish-purple foliage and pink flowers of Geranium 'Pink Spice', herald the entrance to a path. "Now, this is a color you never see in nature, yet it adds a great deal of life," Linda notes. "A burst of high chroma color punches up a garden. And it's easy. Just use a bucket of latex paint. And if you don't like it, paint it again."**

ABOVE, RIGHT: **A curved concrete wall, artfully painted in terra cotta to appear ancient, is the background foil for the most silver-gray of grasses (***Elymus magellanicus***) paired with** *Mertensia asiatica* **and a fountain of burgundy foliage and red-flowering** *Phygelius* **'African Queen'. The burgundy is echoed in** *Beschorneria decosteriana* **and** *Geranium pratense* **'Midnight Reiter'.** BELOW RIGHT: **On the terrace, the same color used on the wall is repeated on the pool ledge and surround. Growing in the water are** *Typha latifolia* **'Variegata', papyrus, and** *Colocasia esculenta.* OPPOSITE, TOP: **Linda sets containers of water in the garden, sometimes planted and sometimes not. The water reflects light and the color of plants, like the yellow of** *Crocosmia* **'Jenny', seeming to add a fourth dimension to the already complex arrangement.** BELOW: **Within a frame of** *Aralia elata* **'Variegata' the view is funneled back to a stand of** *Miscanthus sinensis* **'Cosmopolitan', with its collar of deep red astilbe.**

artists Little and Lewis to appear at once ancient and modern. The artists' concrete sculpture of a blue Meconopsis poppy, set in the pool, drips water, while koi circle underneath.

As if this garden, which covers an acre and a half, were not enough to care for by herself, Linda founded a business, Froggy Bottom Nursery, in 1998. There she divides her own plants, grows infants from seed, and purchases plugs or tissue-cultured plants. (Many patented plants, she points out, can only be acquired from plugs or liners.) In two years her stock has risen to 10,000 plants, which she sells wholesale in the Seattle area.

Linda concentrates on raising hard-to-find plants she has known and grown in her garden. Her nursery list includes *Boehmeria nivea* 'Ramie', a subshrub with textural pleated leaves, the "essential" hardy banana, *Musa basjoo,* and the coveted but tender "red banana" (*Ensete ventricosum* 'Maurelii'), which holds court in the middle of a square of golden variegated *Carex musk-inguemensis* 'Oehme'. By growing quantities of a plant, like the carex, Linda is able to create a mass planting in her own garden—it took fifty plants to fill the square—and to provide stock for her customers who wish to do likewise.

To keep these big plants healthy, Linda feeds them generously. The nursery infants receive weekly doses of liquid fertilizer, and the big eaters out in the garden, like the bananas, receive routine doses. Each year she spreads 100 cubic yards of organic compost throughout the garden. Still, beyond the feeding programs and vigilant watering through the dry summer months, she does not cater to prima donna plants.

Most of Linda's plants require no winter protection. She makes an exception for the hardy banana, which she mounds with leaves; she must dig up the red one. Plants that summer in pots, like the purple-black *Colocasia* 'Black Magic', take up residency through the cold months in a 15-by-40-foot sunroom, which Linda warms with a woodstove. But, the majority of Linda's wonder women and supermen—the cannas, dahlias, gingers, and restios—remain in the ground. She has cast her net for hardy plants with flair and she is always investigating and testing more varieties.

"I don't think I could make a garden without the tropicals and the grasses," she says. "I'm hooked on big, bold, and beautiful. I like dramatic splash."

BIG, BOLD, AND BEAUTIFUL

Plants with a Tropical Flair

Caltapa bignonioides 'Aurea'

BOTANICAL NAME	COMMON NAME	DESCRIPTION
Auralia elata	Japanese angelica tree	Small tree or shrub, 10 to 20 feet with enormous compound leaves to 3 feet long. The variegated forms, both yellow and white, are most desirable. Zone 5.
Canna	Canna lily	Large paddle-shaped leaves, often striped in reds, greens, and yellows. Bright red, pink, and orange flowers. Most cannas are hardy in the ground to at least Zone 8. Otherwise they can be dug up and stored in an unheated garage as rhizomes, making sure they do not freeze or totally dry out.
Dahlia	Dahlia	Many dahlias, particularly those with dark reddish foliage and simple flowers, are good accompaniment to the large, broad leaves of cannas and bananas. Hardy, with mulch cover, to Zone 8. In colder climates, lift tubers, allow to dry upside-down, and store in well-ventilated, frost-free area.
Ensete ventricosum 'Maurelii'	Abyssinian purple banana	Single-trunked banana relative with spectacular large reddish leaves; hardy only to Zone 9, but such a fast grower it is worth treating as a pot plant or annual in colder climates.
Hedychium	Ginger lily	Lance-shaped leaves on erect plants on reed-like stems. Trumpet-shaped, often fragrant flowers in white, yellow, or orange-red. Many are hardy to Zone 7 or 8.
Kniphofia	Red hot pokers	Erect, dense, spike-like racemes. Most are hardy to Zones 6 to 9.
Melianthus major	South African honey flower	One of the most beautiful foliage plants, with highly textural pinnate bluish foliage. Hardy to Zone 7B once established; a superb pot plant in colder climates.
Musa basjoo	Hardy banana	Hardiest banana, to 15 feet tall with multiple trunks. Zone 7 or colder with protection.
Phormium	New Zealand flax	Evergreen, sword-like clumps of leaves in a variety of colors from red to green to yellow with many variegations. Reliably hardy only to Zone 9, but wonderful pot plant in colder zones.
Trachycarpus fortunei	Chinese windmill palm	One of the hardiest palms. It eventually forms a hairy trunk 10 to 20 feet tall. Zone 7 or 8; colder with protection.
	Bamboo	There are bamboos of many different heights, from short to the very tall; not all are runners, seek the clump-forming varieties. Many are surprisingly hardy.

AMBER WAVES
Ornamental Grasses

Elymus magellanicus, paired with *Mertensia asiatica*

BOTANICAL NAME	COMMON NAME	DESCRIPTION
Achnatherum calamagrostis (*Stipa calamagrostis*)	Silver spike grass, silver spear grass	A graceful, long-flowering midsize grass with feathery, luminescent inflorescense. To 3 feet in bloom. Zone 5.
Anemanthele lessoniana (*Stipa arundinacea*)	Pheasant's tail grass, New Zealand wind grass	One of the most beautiful grasses. Makes a clump to 3 feet tall and as wide when mature. Gold and orange tinted foliage moves gracefully in the wind. Not always hardy in Zone 8, but seedlings are usually available as replacements. Makes a superb pot plant.
Carex elata 'Aurea' ('Bowles Golden')	Bowles' golden sedge	Bright yellow leaves with random green stripes. To 2½ feet. Zone 5. Deciduous.
Carex muskinguemensis 'Oehme'	Yellow-variegated palm sedge	Tropical-looking grass with variegated yellow leaves. Zone 4. Deciduous.
Carex secta		Uncommon evergreen sedge. Bright green foliage with a hint of bronze. To 3 feet. Zone 7.
Cortaderia richardii	Toe toe, tussock grass	Pampas grass with better year-round foliage than the more common *Cortaderia selloana*. Plumes near white with a brassy tinge. Base of 4 feet and plumes to 10 feet. Zone 8.
Elymus magellanicus	Blue wheatgrass	Clumping, noninvasive, and tufted. The bluest grass currently available. Grows well in Pacific Northwest, less well where summers are hot and humid. To 1½ feet. Zone 6.
Nasella tenuissima	Mexican feather grass	One of the finest-textured of all ornamental grasses. Straw-colored clump to 2 feet. Drought-tolerant. Zone 6.
Pennisetum orientale 'Tall Tails'	Tall tails fountain grass	One of the best pennisetums, this relatively new cultivar is taller—to 4 feet—than the others. Dense, clump-forming, and more graceful and floriferous. Fluffy white with pink tints. Zone 6.
Stipa gigantea	Giant feather grass	Elegant and stately feather grass. Evergreen basal foliage to 1½ feet with bloom stalks to 8 feet, beginning in June and lasting throughout the rest of the year. Drought-tolerant. Zone 6.

Achnatherum calamagrostis

HIS SEASON IN THE SUN

Dino Anagnost
Germantown, New York

THE MOMENT he arrives from New York City at his upstate weekend retreat, Dino Anagnost jumps out of the car and heads into the gardens that surround the house. Clippers at the ready, he gathers armfuls of flowers. "A house without flowers is a sad house," he says. "I garden to cut flowers for the home."

His taste runs to *big*. No wimpy little petunias or shrinking violets. From May through July he makes do with bold long-stemmed or large-faced flowers, like cosmos, blazing star, zinnia, purple coneflower, monkshood, foxglove, and monarda. But, come late July, August, and September, it's Dino's season: The Season of the Sunflower.

"After all, I'm a Leo," he says, as if that explains the passion perfectly. What other flower could be his signature? "Leo is the lion of the sun."

Dino Anagnost

"I just can't get enough of these magnificent flowers."

In 1988, Dino and two colleagues jointly purchased the historic James Smith Livingston House on the Roeliff Jansen Kill, a 30-foot-wide tributary that empties into the Hudson River in Columbia County. Built in three stages, the building began circa 1690 with a single room, which was probably used as a trading post for the Indian-Dutch fur trade. Subsequent portions of the house were added in the early eighteenth and nineteenth centuries. Members of the prominent Livingston family occupied the house from 1775 until 1913. (Robert Livingston, grandfather of James, had received 166,000 acres on the banks of the Hudson in a land grant from Queen Anne in 1708.)

The house boasts myriad historic features, including a wedding staircase, ceiling beams from Dutch ships, and 2-foot-thick stone walls with buckwheat insulation. A safe house during the Civil War, it has a cave-like room in the basement foundation wall that was used to hide slaves on their way to Canada. Its history was a primary impetus to own the house, and with the other owners Dino has undertaken a careful restoration.

"The potential for gardens here was also a big reason to purchase the place," Dino recalls. "And with three wells on the property, we knew we would have plenty of water." During the summer following the acquisition, Dino staked out his gardens. "There was not one flower on this property when we bought it," he adds.

All that is different now. The maestro—Dino has been the music director and conductor of the Little Orchestra Society in New York since 1980—leads visitors through his garden with the same vigor, energy, and presence that he commands on the podium, pointing out newly planted trees, the cutting gardens, the herb garden, a rose garden, and a garden that hugs the edge of a renovated 1½-acre pond, complete with Versailles-like fountain. All of these are but overtures to the main movement: the sunflower garden.

"I first saw a field of sunflowers in Tuscany, and I was bowled over. But those fields were planted with just one variety. I wanted to take the idea to another level," Dino says. In a ½-acre field that would have made van Gogh think he was in heaven, masses of sunflowers are lined up in eight 50-foot-long, parallel U-shaped beds. The sunflowers range in height from the 12-inch 'Big Smile' to the 12-foot 'Paul Bunyan'; their heads can be as small as 'Maximilian', the size of a half dollar, or swell to the mighty 'Mammoth', in excess of 1 foot in diameter.

"When I started," Dino recalls, "I had no idea of the range of color, texture, and scale in sunflowers. I only knew the old-fashioned standbys, like 'Mammoth'. My first summer I planted four varieties." These days Dino plants forty-five different varieties of sunflowers, from creamy whites through vanilla and sun yellows to red, bronze, and deep burgundy. Lest that number appear to limit the plant's reputation for diversity, he quickly adds, "The genus contains sixty-seven species, native to the Americas—North America, Central America, Peru, and Chile." The showy, daisy-like flowers (members of the Compositae-Asteraceae

PREVIOUS PAGES: **Dino Anagnost has dedicated an entire field to sunflowers. Each weekend in late summer and fall, he gathers masses to grace every table, shelf, or mantel with his signature bouquets. The 6-inch face of a burgundy 'Velvet Queen' prompts Dino to rhapsodize, "Just look at this color!"** ABOVE: **The face of 'Teddy Bear' evokes images of a fuzzy, ancient mask for this gardener.**

family) are borne singly on coarse stalks or in loose corymbs, with the blossoms opening sequentially. The flower is a composite of small florets arranged in circles. Each floret has its own ovary, stigma, style, and anthers and produces a single seed. A flower a foot in diameter can contain as many as eight thousand florets.

Most of the sunflowers Dino grows are annuals derived from *Helianthus annuus*. He does devote one of the huge beds to the perennials *H. maximiliani* and *H. × multiflorus* 'Soleil d'Or', which cascade through and over a rail fence; of those plants, Dino says, "The more you cut, the more they bloom."

"I plant about four thousand seeds each year," he says. "A thousand for the deer, a thousand for the birds, a thousand that I may lose, and a thousand to cut." He plots out a planting plan

"Sunflowers," Dino says, "will last eight to ten days as cut flowers." He advises cutting long stems in the garden, and then cutting as needed on a slant. Six to eight inches from the end he makes light incisions on the stem with a flower knife to help the stalk take up water quickly after the shock of being cut.

on yellow lined paper indicating the expected height of each variety. His system is simple. In the spring he rototills each 4-foot-wide bed. "This field had horses for twenty-five years, so I really don't need to add anything. However, I would suggest that someone who did not inherit a meadow of black gold should top-dress with well-rotted manure or compost." When all danger of frost is past, he direct-sows the seeds by hand every 6 inches in straight rows 8 inches apart, horizontally across the beds. Depending on the variety, germination occurs in eight to fourteen days with flowering from fifty-five days to seventy-five days after planting.

Dino built a greenhouse for housing his collection of tender plants through the winter. An added benefit is the possibility of both accelerating and extending his sunflower season. Dino says, "Sunflowers can be given a head start in a greenhouse and planted out after germination, or when the soil stays at about 65°F. By staggering the greenhouse plantings about a week apart, an even longer blooming season can be achieved."

He acknowledges that thinning the seedlings, when they are 4 to 6 inches high, is recommended, but he does not do it. His plants seem to thrive in close quarters. He waters for the first couple of weeks, if necessary. After that the plants are on their own. "They thrive in hot sunny weather, and they do like a well-drained site; wet feet will not please them." Dino does not bother to weed between the plants, because, as he says, "these superplants can outperform most weeds." He also theorizes that the weed blanket discourages the deer from making appetizers of the sunflower seedlings.

Dino's 1,000-plus plants make a majestic show, with different varieties vying for attention as they come into bloom throughout the summer's end. Most stay in bloom for five to six weeks. "Some years I've even had them through November." Seeking the spectacular is part of the sport. Sunflowers hybridize freely, and may not come true from seed. Dino has begun to collect seeds from his favorites, however, hoping to select a superior strain— "the bigger, the better, the richer the color. The bees love these flowers. You'll see a half-dozen bees feasting on one round face. They are hard at work pollinating. And I'd love some fine new sunny face to emerge from this garden."

Not even as ebullient a flower arranger as Dino can exhaust the quantity of his crop. Throughout his home the focus of each room or porch table is a great bouquet. Even the vessels are chosen with exuberance: Italian ceramics, antique pewter, wood, copper, old watering cans. "I'm always thinking containers," Dino admits. Some arrangements are exclusively sunflowers; others admit minor characters from the cutting garden. While Dino doesn't worry about pollen on his dining room table, he admits that some pollen does stain. For those who do care, he suggests seeking some of the new pollenless hybrids, crosses between *Helianthus annuus* and *H. petiolaris*. Dino particularly likes 'Sunrich Lemon' and 'Sunrich Orange', but he also plants pollenless hybrid mixes like 'Parasol Mix' and 'Fun 'n Sun' for their varieties in size and color.

At summer's end the great sunflower heads fall down under their own weight and the effects of frost. Dino leaves them on the ground as fare for the birds until spring, when they are carted to the compost pile. Winter is not devoid of the pleasure of their company, however. During his travels and his engagements with the internationally active orchestra, Dino has collected hand-colored French, English, German, Italian, and American botanical prints of sunflowers. The prints date from the seventeenth to the late nineteenth century and grace the walls of all the rooms. Sunflowers beam from trays and towels, mugs and plates. One is inlaid on an early German table. Even on the darkest day the house is alive with golden orbs. "They're happy. They smile at you. My colors are blue and yellow. The sunflowers are a thousand suns against the sky."

OPPOSITE, LEFT TO RIGHT: **Dino adores sunflowers in all their stages, from opening bud to drooping seed head. "Just watch the bud unfurl,"** he says of 'Happy Face'. TOP: **The floriferous perennials** *Helianthus maximilliani*

and *H.* × *multiflorus* 'Soleil d'Or' tumble through the fence that separates the sunflower field from the rest of the garden. ABOVE: Dino adds, "Look at the gorgeous honeycomb structure of the seed head of the giant 'Mammoth'."

THE SUN KING'S FAVORITE SUBJECTS

Sunflowers

VARIETY*	FLOWER SIZE	COLOR	PLANT HEIGHT
Autumn Beauty	7 inches	Variegated red and yellow	7 feet
Aztec Gold	11 inches	Yellow; edible seeds	6 feet
Big Smile	5 inches	Golden yellow	1½ to 2 feet
Chianti Hybrid	3 to 4 inches	Burgundy-red with touch of gold, pollenless	4 to 5 feet
De Sol Hybrid	8 to 10 inches	Bright yellow, deep brownish black center, pollenless	5 feet
Double Sun Gold	6 inches	Extra fuzzy, golden, green center	4 to 5 feet
Ebony & Gold	5 inches	Golden, black eye	5 to 6 feet
Elf	4 inches	Yellow	14 to 16 inches
Endurance *Helianthus argophyllus* × *annuus*	4 to 6 inches	Bright yellow petals, small center	6 to 9 feet
Evening Sun	8 to 10 inches	Maroon petals, red-black center	6 to 9 feet
Floristan	6 inches	Unusual bicolor with rusty-red petals with yellow tips, dark center	3 feet
Fun 'n Sun Hybrid Mix	3 to 8 inches	Single and double flowers in red, gold, yellow, bicolor; pollenless	4 to 6 feet
Inca Jewels	6 inches	Bright yellow, banded in gold, orange, and burgundy	5 to 10 feet
Indian Blanket Hybrid	4 inches	Single and semidouble bicolor, wine-red with lemon-yellow-tipped petals	4 to 5 feet
Israeli	10 to 14 inches	Golden	4 to 6 feet
Italian White *Helianthus debilis* subsp. *Cucumerifolius*	3 inches	Creamy white, black center	4 feet
Japanese Silverleaf *Helianthus argophyllus*	3 to 4 inches	Bright yellow, silver foliage	5 to 6 feet
Gloriosa Polyheaded	4 to 6 inches	Straw-yellow and brilliant orange, red markings, resembles Gloriosa Daisy	6 to 8 feet
Golden Pheasant	8 inches	Orange-yellow, densely petaled	4 to 6 feet
Hallo	6 to 8 inches	Golden-yellow, dark center	5 to 6 feet
Happy Face	5 inches	Golden-yellow, greenish yellow center	9 to 12 feet
Holiday	6 to 8 inches	Golden-yellow, dark center	4 feet
Kid Stuff	10 inches	Golden-yellow	32 inches
Lemon Éclair Hybrid	6 to 8 inches	Lemon-yellow double, brown center; pollenless	4 to 6 feet
Mammoth	12 to 14 inches	Old-fashioned yellow, dark center	9 to 12 feet
Maximilian *Helianthus maximiliani*, prairie sunflower, perennial	2 inches	Golden-yellow	7 feet
Moonshadow Hybrid	4 inches	Pale yellow petals fading to creamy white, dark centers; pollenless	4 feet
Moonwalker	6 to 8 inches	Soft, creamy pale yellow	8 to 10 feet

Music Box	4 inches	Creamy yellow to mahogany red with black center	2½ feet
Parasol Mix	3 to 8 inches	Yellow, gold, burgundy, red, bicolor; pollenless	3 to 5 feet
Paul Bunyan	12 inches	Yellow, supplies seeds for songbirds	13 to 15 feet
Prado Red	6 inches	Deep garnet red	3½ to 4 feet
Red Sun	3 to 4 inches	Red petals, red center	5 to 6 feet
Russian Giant	10 inches	Yellow	11 feet
Soleil d'Or *Helianthus* × *multiflorus,* perennial	3 to 4 inches	Double yellow	5 feet
Sonja	4 inches	Golden-orange, dark center	3 to 4 feet
Sunbeam	6 to 8 inches	Golden-yellow ray petals, center disc of yellow-green; the van Gogh look-alike sunflower; pollenless	5 feet
Sunbright	5 inches	Golden-yellow, brown center; pollenless	4 to 6 feet
Sundance Kid	4 to 5 inches	Semidouble bronze and golden-yellow, tufted or crested center	18 inches
Sundrops	3 inches	Golden-yellow, dark center	4 to 5 feet
Sun Gold	8 inches	Double, chrysanthemum-like, golden-yellow	4 to 5 feet

Sunrich Lemon	10 inches	Lemon-yellow, black center; pollenless	4 to 6 feet
Sunrich Orange	10 inches	Deep golden-orange; pollenless	4 to 6 feet
Sunrise	6 inches	Lemon-yellow	5 feet
Sunspot	12 inches	Yellow	1½ to 2 feet
Tangina	4 inches	Deep orange, dark center	3 feet
Tarahumara White Shelled	8 inches	Solid gold	7 feet
Teddy Bear	8 inches	Extra-double, gold	2 feet
Tithonia Sundance	2 inches	Scarlet-orange	4 feet
Tithonia Torch	2 inches	Red-orange	4 feet
Valentine	6 inches	Lemon-yellow, dark brown center	5 feet
Vanilla Ice	6 inches	Pale lemon-yellow, brown center	5 feet
Velvet Queen	6 inches	Deep red, bronze, chestnut	6 to 8 feet

Helianthus annuus, unless otherwise noted.

STAIRWAY TO HEAVEN

Jack C. Miller
Collegeville, Pennsylvania

"This," Jack Miller reflects, sweeping his arms to encompass the Asian style he has absorbed so completely, "is what I was meant to do." Jack bends forward as he steps through a 5-foot-high opening in the Humble Gate, a traditional Japanese conceit that forces the visitor to bow in respect to the garden and its master. Inside the garden, the atmosphere is tranquil, elegant, seemingly ancient. The earth, contoured in mounds, is draped with a tapestry of moss woven in shades from chartreuse to deep blue-green. Jack believes his moss—about twenty-five different genera – to be the largest private collection in America.

Paths wend their way back and forth up a gentle slope toward a gazebo. "As in the Japanese tradition of stroll gardens, it takes 70 feet of path to move a distance of 20 feet," Jack says. The Rainbow

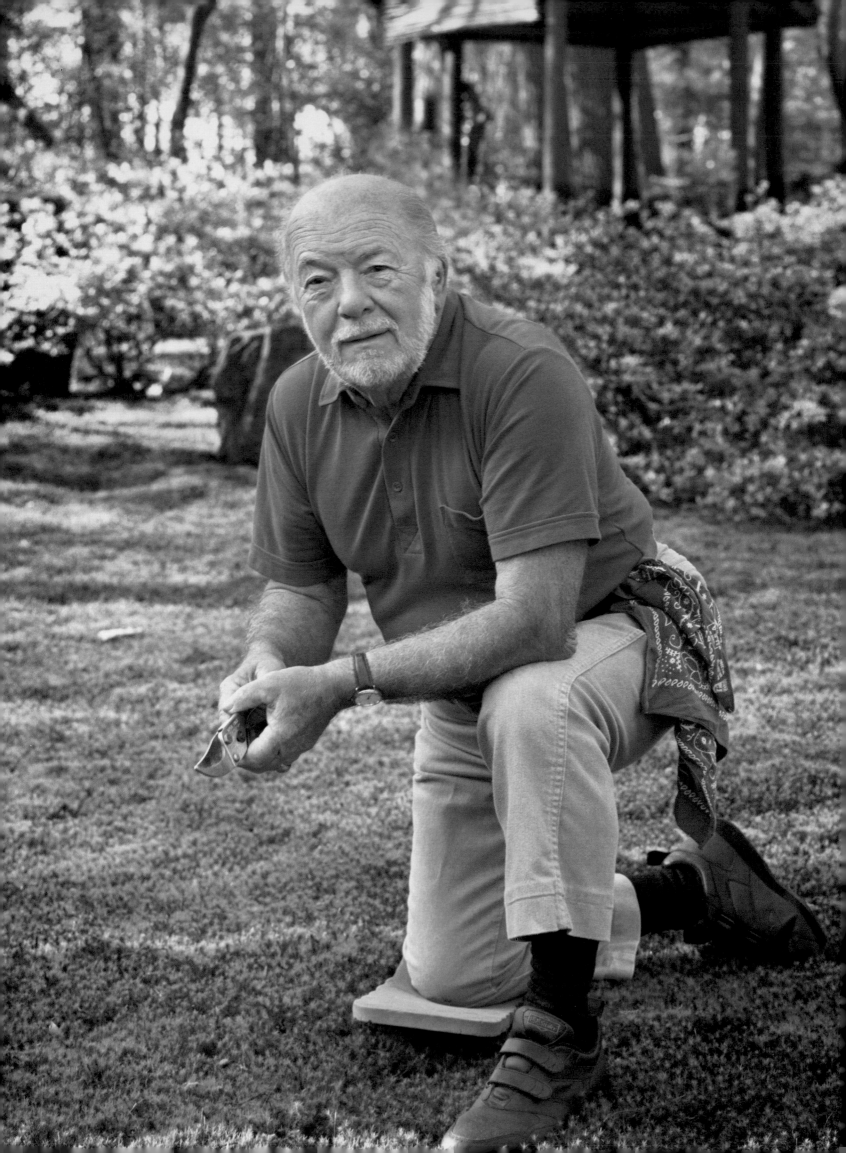

Jack C. Miller

"A Japanese garden is filled with quiet mystery."

Bridge, a 22-foot-long arc, spans a rock-lined dry pool with a gravel riverbed. By design the bridge is too steep to walk over, an allusion to the difficult passage from this world to paradise.

Stones, chosen for "their soul," are placed with instinctual grace throughout the blanket of moss. Some with rounded tops suggest turtles, a symbol of the timeless quality of the garden. A "homemade" mushroom or a lantern, which illuminates the way, has been added under a tree or beside a gate. In a dry stone basin by the front door, water is represented by crushed gravel; it symbolizes the ritual of guests' purification of the body and soul. A connoisseur of trees and shrubs as well as stone, Jack selects plants with presence—mugo pines, Japanese maples, and rhododendrons—and prunes them to further elaborate on their natural forms.

"This," Jack says with passion, "is the only piece of land I have ever owned." When he

PREVIOUS PAGES: **Two decades ago, Jack Miller had an epiphany. "I orientalized my garden," he says. "In my head it happened overnight. In actuality, it took twenty-two years."** LEFT: **The Humble Gate.** RIGHT: **the Rainbow Bridge.** THIS PAGE, BELOW: **The**

bought it in the early 1950s "we couldn't even see lights from any other house." He designed the Chester County sandstone house, located about 25 miles northwest of Philadelphia, and worked alongside the mason as the building took shape. For years Jack was on the road, in the business of the artificial breeding of dairy cows. While he owned 3½ acres, he gardened only in the immediate vicinity of the house, as leisure time was at a premium. To enhance his home Jack added plants, placing them in the "American tradition of foundation planting, where plants get too big in fifteen years and have to be removed." Incorporated into his present garden are many fifty-year-old shrubs—boxwood, Glenn Dale azaleas, Japanese holly (*Ilex crenata*), *I. c.* 'Helleri', *Rhododendron maximum*—which, even then, he chose with a discerning eye. But his garden—and he laughs at it even being called a garden back in those days—was "ordinary."

roofed Front Gate, with a 6-foot section of woven fencing on either side, suggests enclosure. While there is no fence around the property, stepping through the gate removes the visitor from the outside world.

Jack follows the formulas of Japanese garden design, frequently speaking of rhythm, movement, harmony, unity, form, and content. Moss, evergreens, sand, gravel, and stone are his materials of choice, and juxtapositions of opposites—coarse and fine textures, light and dark, ornaments and plants, horizontal and vertical—reinforce a sense of balance. The hard surface of rock contrasts with the vast cushion of soft moss.

Jack says he often learns from serendipity. "I back into things." After he retired in 1971, he began to clear the overgrown slope, a 30-degree incline, to the east of his house. It was almost impenetrable, thatched with vines. Attacking an 8-foot square at a time, it took Jack six or seven years to climb the 225 feet to the site where the gazebo now stands at the highest point. "I could not have done it all at once, or we would have had serious erosion," Jack notes. As a precaution, he dug trenches across the top and down the sides to handle the runoff.

Because the land was graced with a mature 125-foot canopy of red oak, hickory, ironwood, sassafras, and tulip poplar, the slightly acid clay soil was covered with 4 inches of leaf mold, top-dressed with a couple of inches of dried leaves. Out of curiosity, Jack removed the mold and the leaves.

By exposing the clay to light and oxygen, Jack inadvertently set the scene for the arrival of moss. Spores, which had been inactive under the thick blanket of leaves, sprang to life and began to multiply. Others arrived on the wind. Within months mosses blanketed the landscape. Jack was immediately drawn to the texture and richness of the carpet, which he saw as an alternative to conventional lawn. He encouraged its growth, and when Mother Nature was too slow for his taste, he scouted the riverbanks in the Perkiomen Creek valley for moss specimens, which he gathered and smoothed into place. He says proudly that he has never "bought a dollar's worth of moss." He augmented the woodland with more native plants: jack-in-the-pulpit, mayapple, Solomon's seal, partridge berry (*Mitchella repens*), pipsissewa (*Chimaphila maculata*), and colonies of ferns.

In 1978, Jack met Hiroshi Makita, a Japanese garden designer, who had been trained in a Zen Buddhist monastery and who worked in the Philadelphia area. At their first encounter, Hiroshi recounted his frustration that a garden he was creating was resisting the transplanting of moss. Jack said, "Come visit me. I've got moss."

Hiroshi came—and stayed. The setting, the moss, and Jack's open and inquisitive mind were an irresistible welcome, not to mention the hospitality of a warm home. The Millers offered Hiroshi living quarters in exchange for design and gardening work, an arrangement that lasted for five years. That period fueled Jack's transformation from apprentice to master.

The two men worked together, with Jack absorbing theory and practice. "Hiroshi made sure that everything we did was pure to the Japanese way," Jack recalls. With the dedication of a passionate collector, Jack studied Japanese culture and gardens. "I read everything."

Jack maintains that Zen teachings are important to understanding the aesthetics of Japanese gardening. Zen gardens are created to facilitate contemplation during meditation; their features are to be realized through the powers of suggestion and symbolism. In the interests of self-discipline, even austerity, few flowers are welcome. "Their colors are considered gaudy. We never plant daisies, hollyhocks, or cannas," Jack says. Color comes from the spring-blooming azaleas and the delicate hues of the Japanese maples. The palette is subtle. "Sometimes," Jack concedes, "even the flowering azaleas are too much."

The landscape is punctuated with stone, either singly or in complex arrangement. By defying realistic scale, by simplifying a design to its essence, Jack can make a group of stones evoke a monumental mountain waterfall or a tiny stream just emerging from its source. Another abstract grouping suggests an irregular pool of water. There is no water anywhere in Jack's garden. He works only in the dry landscape tradition called *karesansui*. One of the most important design principles, he says, is the one-third to two-thirds ratio of placement in the hardscaping. "When setting two rocks of differing sizes together, I put the smaller one off to the side using that ratio," he instructs. "It is the key to asymmetrical balance."

There are no straight lines here, he continues, pointing to small details, like the sides of the opening in the Front Gate, one of the first pieces of garden architecture Jack and Hiroshi built together. While the structure is exactingly constructed, one of the upright posts is perfectly straight; the other, embellished with the trunk of an Osage orange tree, is slightly curved. That bend gives the opening a subtle rhythm that pleases the eye.

A Japanese garden requires skillful pruning. A plant's size and shape determine its harmony with the whole. As Jack passes the curved head of a red pine (*Pinus densiflora* 'Yokashuka'), he

Jack says, "When a rock is placed the right way, the rock speaks to you. I believe it has spirit. It says yes." LEFT: The mountain waterfall. BELOW: A dry stream source. BOTTOM: The dry stone basin by the front door.

A MANTLE OF MOSS

Luxury Underfoot

SOME 400 million years old, moss is a quiet but determined survivor. Still low in the hierarchy of living things, it produces no flowers. It spreads by root-like extensions of its stem, called rhizoids, and depending on the species, it either travels across wide areas, encompassing everything in its path, or contains itself in neat little mounds. It can be notoriously willful, even elusive; it will move at its own pace. Yet Jack Miller has encouraged a remarkable range of native mosses to blanket 2 acres of his garden.

Moss requires a hard surface, like clay or stone, to

thrive, and Jack's garden provides both. He points out that if conditions are good, chances are, the moss was an inhabitant of the area before "progress" drove the luxuriant green mantle into hiding. Moss reproduces by spores, tiny motes that float on currents of air or water across continents and oceans. Spores may reside in the soil, waiting to come to life, if given the welcome sign.

Jack's clay-like soil is slightly acidic—it has a pH of between 5 and 6, which is to moss's taste—though Jack cautions against making too much of acid versus

alkaline. Moss requires excellent drainage, and where the slope of Jack's garden was not sufficient, he created mounds, like little hillocks with gradual runoff on all four sides. An established moss garden also likes some sun. Jack's high tree canopy allows the sun to moderate the ground temperature during the cool weather and filter the scorching sun during July and August. "A canopy that filters about 50 percent is ideal," he says.

When Jack wants to move moss, he does it in the spring or fall. Young moss, "as immature as you can handle, perhaps only one-half-inch thick, is much easier to transplant than more mature growths." He uses a flat shovel about 8 inches wide, which he slides under the moss to lift it gingerly.

The new location should be "firm and moist, not cookie-crumb humus. People make the mistake of trying to plant moss on rich humus, which is the worst thing." Disturbing the "almost negligible roots" as little as possible, Jack eases the transplant into place and pats it gently. He mists the newly placed moss, rather than watering with a hose, as the transplanted moss is easily displaced. Once the moss is established, it requires no maintenance. Jack does not water or fertilize. "Moss is tough," he says. "You can walk on it, as long as you don't walk over the same spot repeatedly. And never walk on it during the dry months, when it becomes powdery and fragile."

Moss does, however, take vigilant weeding. "Nothing is a better medium for propagating seeds than moss." Though Jack allows certain native woodland plants to grow through the moss, including little colonies of dwarf fern, Solomon's seal, or pipsissewa. He is always in control, watching for an invasion, which he nips immediately. Unpredictable, aggressive plants have been banished. The tiny blue Quaker lady (*Hedyotis caerulea*), or bluet, which he concedes is charming, pops up frequently and must be plucked at once. "Give up for a year, and you've got a bluet garden. Choose what you want. A bluet garden or a moss garden. It's that simple."

Robins churn up the moss like miniature rototillers, as they seek moisture and worms. Squirrels scruff the surface looking for nuts, and they create havoc out of sheer devilment. Yet this moss garden, after two decades, seems secure as well as serenely beautiful. And, as Jack observes, "The more moss you have, the more you will have."

BOTANICAL NAME · COMMON NAME · DESCRIPTION

BOTANICAL NAME	COMMON NAME	DESCRIPTION
Amblystegium		All genera are very similar; finely textured, mat-forming, dark green; inhabiting moist logs and tree bases
Atrichum undulatum	Star moss	Upright tufts; new growth is bright, light green, which darkens with age; spore capsule is a dense flock of green cormorant heads on curved necks with reddish stems. Seeks newly disturbed soil; forms handsome green patches in fallow areas; transplant with care, as clumps break apart easily
Aulacomnium palustre		Pale greenish yellow in spring; in summer appearing more bleached or golden; must be kept moist, easily transplanted
Bryum argenteum	Bryum moss	Leaf is silvery green; grows easily between garden pavers; easily transplanted; withstands drought
Bryum capillare	Bryum	Like green velvet; compact ground cover; survives in soils of low fertility
Climacium dendroides	Tree moss, umbrella moss	Arboreal heads 2 to 3 inches tall; long, tapered tips of leaves; likes moist soil along stream beds or on damp rotting logs in shade or sun; dig deep when transplanting
Climacium americanum	Tree moss, umbrella moss	Twin to *C. dendroides*, but leaf tips are more ovate
Dicranella heteromala		Velvety fine and dense; grows in tufts and patches; grows on sunny stream banks and roadsides; volunteers in woodsy gardens
Dicranum scoplium		Stiff, needle-like leaves in pale green or gold; deep sturdy mat; likes shade
Ditrichum heteromallum	Ditrichum moss	Yellow-green, erect, broomy of leaf; common in lawns in summer
Encalypta ciliata		Tufts of dark green; hooded spore case looks like a candle snuffer; likes rockeries
Entodon		Thick mats, deep green or shiny gold-green; likes boulders and tree trunks
Funaria hygrometrica	Interloper moss	Forms low-growing mats of minute tufty branches; spore cases are pear-shaped and orange; very showy; arrives in greenhouse plants; difficult to transplant
Hygrohypnum luridum		Mat-forming; densely overlaps horizontal branches; likes moist shade
Hylocomium spendens	Feather moss, fern moss	Downy, wispy fronds; grows on moist forest floor in leaf mold
Hypnum cupressiforme	Plume moss	Mat-forming, fringe-like, olive-green; hangs from bark or boulders
Leptobryum pyriforme	Pavement moss	Minute hair-like deep green leaves; resembles animal fur; finds fallow edges of garden paths, coats moist concrete
Leucobryum albidum; L. glaucum	Pincushion or white moss	Firm, dense colonies like hummocks; sends out flat extensions from central hump, produces a wavy effect; greenish bluish white when dry, light green after rain
Pohlia wahlenbergii	Carpet moss	Fine green plush; makes large stretches of cover; whitish when dry; bluish green when moist
Polytrichum commune; P. juniperandum; P. piliferum	Haircap moss	Large family of tufted fur-like needles around wiry stems; perhaps tallest moss in America; dark green with "splash caps" on male plants; easy to transplant; likes moisture
Rhytidiadelphus loreus		Recurved leaves, soft green; likes shade; easy to transplant; will take over grass
Rhytidiadelphus squarrosus		Soft green; takes over lawns; makes an alternative to lawns; needs no mowing; prolific ground cover
Sphagnum imbricatum	Peat moss	Mat-forming rosettes of densely packed branches facing upward; orange, yellow, and yellow-green; likes sunny moist areas; dislikes heavily chlorinated water
Thuidium delicatulum	Feather moss; fern moss	Large frondy moss, looks like feathers or fern; grows well in deep woods with high humidity
Tortula muralis		Tufting, cushioning moss with small hairy leaves that end in points; inhabits concrete and brick walls

stops to "candle" it—nipping off the candles—a ritual he performs each spring to keep it in proportion to the entrance gate. Keeping plants under control sometimes means guiding them to grow contrary to their nature. An *Ilex* × 'Nelly R. Stevens' spills over a wall, forming another green waterfall. Jack says, "I whacked off its leaders every time it grew them. It got the message. It doesn't produce leaders anymore."

Jack surveys his accomplishment. "The ironic thing is that I have never even been to Japan," he says. "The closest I came was being on a hospital ship in Yokohama harbor after the war in 1946." Carmen, his wife, interjects, "When Japanese visitors come to the garden, they bow to

OPPOSITE: **Two Japanese maples (***Acer palmatum atropurpureum* **'Crimson Queen') form a living gate, their limbs trained to connect overhead.** LEFT: **A**

Juniperus procumbens **'Nana' planted at the top of a wall flows straight down at the speed of a glacier to form a green waterfall.** RIGHT: **The Stairway to Heaven.**

Jack. They say he has been to Japan in another lifetime." While Jack has taken Japanese principles and made them his own, he often interpreted concepts, like the suggestions of mountains, oceans, islands, and waterfalls, in his own fashion. "I have taken liberties."

Jack looks up the steps, a series of seventeen broad stone slabs that lead to the Millers' front door. They are placed in a configuration of the double *S* curve, one more formula that Jack has learned, revered, and used repeatedly. "This is what I call the Stairway to Heaven," he says, smiling. Perhaps it is a metaphor for the creation of his garden.

MAJESTIES

Marlyn Sachtjen
Waunakee, Wisconsin

MARLYN SACHTJEN, an energetic woman no more than 5 feet
2 inches tall, is a crusader. Her enemy: "Green velvet," the term she
applies to that fixture of the suburban landscape—lawn—and the
harmful chemicals required to maintain its lush perfection. "I want
to rid the world of it all," she states emphatically. As Marlyn grew
older and, she claims, wiser, trees, particularly the great and venerable ones, took a more powerful place in her imagination. "I am
now planting a forest," says Marlyn, "and I feel it is one of the most
important things I can do in my lifetime. I believe anyone, no matter
the size of his or her property, can do the same."

Marlyn has restored about one-third of her 5-acre parcel of
land to native midwestern prairie. Numerous prairies—and she
refers to them in the plural, even though they may be as small as 50

Marlyn Sachtjen

"I am planting a forest for my grandchildren—and their grandchildren."

square feet—are scattered throughout her property. Some, well established, are now almost twenty-five years old. On the other two-thirds of her land Marlyn is planting a grand forest of "trees with majesty." The forest is ten years old, and it is the place where her heart now resides. As the trees mature and form a canopy over the land, sun-loving perennials, the interim tapestry of color, will disappear. The more subtle mayapple, fern, uvularia, and Jacob's ladder will take their place. The contrast between the open, undulating stretches of native forbs and grasses and the clusters of trees is dramatic. Through an artful arrangement of paths, the transitions are harmonious, even logical. The planting of prairie and forest, however, was not always Marlyn's way of gardening.

In the 1960s and early 1970s Marlyn was known throughout the Madison, Wisconsin, area for creating magnificent perennial and herb gardens. She recalls, "I was a traditional gardener and proud of what I had accomplished."

In 1976, however, Marlyn attended a lecture that changed her gardening philosophy forever. The subject was prairie restoration. As slides were projected, she recognized the plants, one after another. "I have that," she murmured to herself, "and that, and that, too." At home, she walked down to a rocky corner of her land, which, because of its rough topography had been ignored for two centuries by the farmers, and discovered that she had inherited a treasure: a small piece of original, untouched prairie. Marlyn counted twenty-eight different species growing on that plot, including leadplant (*Amorpha canescens*), tall meadow rue (*Thalictrum polygamum*), and wild bergamot (*Monarda fistulosa*). "It was only about 40 feet square," she says. "But it was real. I instantly fell under the spell of prairie fever." While Marlyn's conversion was swift, the process of changing the complexion of her land took a quarter of a century, "one step at a time."

Marlyn and her late husband, William Sachtjen, loved their land; it was a bonding passion. They had met in Newark, New Jersey, where both were engaged in the war effort. Marlyn says, "I was making bombs, and Bill was working in the Office of Dependency Benefits. I had some secretarial skills and was moved to his office." She was nineteen; he was twenty-seven.

PREVIOUS PAGES, LEFT: **For Marlyn Sachtjen to include a tree in her list of "majesties," it must have bark with character, like the superior variety of green ash, 'Marshall's Seedless'.** RIGHT: **Marlyn refers to native prairies as the Midwest's Gardens of Eden.** THIS PAGE, BELOW: **"Two of the most important requirements for making a prairie are undisturbed soil and regular burning," says Marlyn, and beginning around Thanksgiving, she burns "every day of the winter as long as there is no snow. The ash warms the soil, which prompts germination reaction in many seeds." Marlyn's experiences of returning her land to prairie and forest is documented in her delightful and informative handbook,** *Marlyn's Garden: Seasoned Advice for Achieving Spectacular Results in the Midwest.*

They married at the end of World War II and returned to Wisconsin, Bill's home state.

In 1960 the young couple purchased a 100-by-600-foot parcel of farmland 8 miles northeast of Madison. Set on a gentle hillside, it faces the Yahara River, which empties into Lake Mendota, the largest of Madison's three lakes. Over the years, the Sachtjens purchased a dozen more identically shaped plots.

From the beginning both Marlyn and Bill gardened. While Marlyn leaned toward ornamental plants, Bill grew vegetables for thirty summers, filling one of the 100-by-600-foot sections with a monumental garden. The couple also developed broad sweeps of lawn. "Bill loved to mow; he had headlights on his tractor so he could mow at night," she recalls. Marlyn shudders when she remembers that in keeping their property in rigorous order, "We did all the wrong things. Without knowing. We thought we were being so good to the land. You can't make velvet lawns like that without chemicals. And, I am ashamed to say we used them all."

As Marlyn got swept up in the prairie movement, she began to have misgivings about the

TOP: **White racemes of the native false white indigo (*Baptisia alba*).** ABOVE: **Forest and prairie overlap in a powerful harmony of design. Marlyn says ruefully of her passion, "I'm not sure I've won one person over yet. But I refuse to be defeated. All of a sudden, I think this effort will turn into a ball roller, and everyone will be planting forests."** OPPOSITE: **Marlyn's Shady Lane leads by a collection of achillea past *Pyrus* 'Aristocrat' into a 300-by-100-foot forest.**

chemicals being put into soil and water and the potential damage to wildlife. "I was horrified that we had ever added chemicals to our land," she says. At the same time, the vegetable garden was becoming a burden rather than a pleasure. Marlyn says, "We invited people to come and harvest, but they didn't want to do the work. They were happy to accept the vegetables if we'd pick them and deliver them to their doors. One day Bill said, 'Enough. Let's stop the vegetable garden and plant a forest.'"

Though Bill passed away five months later, Marlyn had already mentally converted the vegetable garden into a forest; its image was imprinted in her mind's eye. The first order of business was to eradicate the lawns. She smothered the turf and weeds with cast-off pieces of wall-to-wall carpeting laid facedown on the ground—an unorthodox antidote to herbicides. The notion "just came to me one day. The carpets kill everything underneath," Marlyn reports with satisfaction. "I've used so many, they would stretch from here to New York City." Their unsightly presence does not faze Marlyn. "I turn them upside down, so you can't see their awful colors. And they work."

Marlyn began to educate herself about trees, just as she had taught herself to recognize prairie natives. When the Sachtjens first moved to their land, a friend had given Bill three hundred saplings—one hundred each of black spruce, white spruce, and Norway pine—

TOP LEFT: **It takes about a year for the carpets, which Marlyn uses to suppress all growth underneath, to deal permanent death to unwanted plants. Since they have a burlap base, they ultimately break down into the earth.** TOP RIGHT: **With paths in place and plants flourishing, Marlyn's unique carpet method of cleansing the land is no longer visible.** ABOVE: **Marlyn has dedicated her efforts at reforesting the land to her late husband, who was an attorney and a circuit judge.**

which the couple planted throughout their land. Another friend had provided some oaks to plant at the perimeter of Marlyn's prairie. Working with these trees as her foundation, she began to add and subtract.

"My tastes changed," Marlyn reflects, and many of the spruce, "trees that grow too densely," have been removed. "As part of a more enlightened approach to tree selection, I now choose trees with majesty. They must have grand structure. And they must be prunable or maintain natural habits that allow me to have vistas through the forest. My vote goes to the oaks, beeches, and chestnuts. Those are the ones I am planting for future generations."

As Marlyn designs her forests, she works one 100-foot-square section at a time. She makes a master plan with a sketch of the layout and a balanced plant selection that combines deciduous trees, shrubs, conifers, and perennial plants. The plan is reworked numerous times, but once a plant is situated, Marlyn never transplants. "I leave a plant where I put it. I let it settle in and have a good life without disturbing it."

Paths are the first features to be installed; the property now boasts 1.8 miles of meandering paths. "I lay out the carpets to form the paths. If I don't like a particular curve or sweep, it's easy to change: just pick up the carpet and move it." When she is satisfied, Marlyn covers the carpets with a layer of coarse wood chips, making the rugs disappear. The path's underlayer of carpet suppresses existing weeds and keeps future ones at bay; it anchors the path and keeps the ground soft and spongy underfoot.

Paths in place, the rest of the section is then carpeted, and Marlyn begins to plant her babies. She makes an opening in the carpeted ground by pulling the rug back, or just slicing a hole in it. Some trees are tiny saplings, purchased from mail-order nurseries. "I like them small. It is easy for me to dig the hole and plant, and the trees will acclimate better this way. I have the pleasure of watching every stage of their growth."

During an infant's first year, Marlyn keeps it watered and mulched to maintain the moisture. "Then it's on its own. No coddling goes on here. I have wonderful, if heavy, soil. Remember, this was a farm. And we spent a good deal of time revitalizing the soil by planting green manure and feeding its nutrients back into the earth. I don't need to fertilize again."

Many more trees are planted from seed, right in place. "I scratch up the ground with a claw, which adds oxygen to the soil, then place the seed or the nut right in the spot where I want it to grow." Marlyn's success rate is remarkable. She recently planted a hundred chestnuts; twenty-five of them grew. "Not a bad percentage," she observes. A glorious 35-foot dogwood, *Cornus florida,* not considered hardy in Waunakee's Zone 4 climate, grew from a seed Marlyn collected at the Menninger Clinic in Kansas, which is in Zone 5. "When I grow a tree from seed, it has no idea that it is not supposed to grow here, and since it starts in the ground, it is not adjusting to a different climate, like those that arrive from nurseries around the country. While the dogwood is considered a sub-tree, or an understory tree, to me it, too, is a majesty. I bow to it each time I walk by." Her eyes sparkle. "Since this system of classification was invented by me, I can call any tree I want a majesty."

A number of other trees Marlyn denotes as "tweeners," those that fall somewhere between undesirables and true majesties, but lean toward the magisterial group if they are "glorious performers." *Pyrus* 'Aristocrat', now 40 feet tall with foliage that flutters in the wind, stands between Marlyn's kitchen window and the vast open farmland. It has persistent red fruit all winter that ferments by spring, causing the feasting birds to behave as if they have indulged in a "drunken orgy." A handsome small specimen tree, *Acer tataricum* 'Red Wings' produces huge

bouquets of winged red fruit. *Prunus maackii,* the Amur chokecherry, wears a cinnamon-colored, exfoliating bark that seems to glow from within. Marlyn stationed a *Pinus densiflora* 'Pendula' outside her bedroom window, where it sways rhythmically in the breeze.

Mother Nature's helping hand has played an active role in the reforestation of Marlyn's property, too. After another section was cleared, using the same carpet scheme, hundreds of native redbuds and river birches emerged. "The seeds had been sleeping there, just waiting who knows how many years for their chance to grow. What a powerful message that sends," says Marlyn. Squirrels are also Marlyn's allies. Like Brownies performing good deeds in the night, they deposit nuts, particularly those from oaks they bring from a nearby grove. Marlyn muses, "From small creatures, whether animal or human, great forests grow."

TOP: *Acer tutaricus* 'Red Wings'. ABOVE, LEFT TO RIGHT: Marlyn's first garden—alpine plants nestled into a berm—is now surrounded entirely by forest and prairie; one of the most distinguished features of Marlyn's conifer garden is a *Pinus densiflora* 'Pendula', which produces large, decorative cones.

COATS OF MANY COLORS
Deciduous Trees of Majesty

MARLYN'S PASSION for trees is rooted in practicality. She considers the season of the wind, a fifth season in the Midwest. The only way to garden in the Heartland, she claims, is to create barriers against the desiccating and damaging force of the wind—in the form of protection belts or windbreaks. That is accomplished with trees and shrubs, carefully selected and planted in staggered rows. The windbreak acts as a climate conditioner, protecting the garden from winter storms and scorching summer sun. In addition, many shrubs and understory trees flower in the spring and supply fruit and berries for the birds, which, in turn, help to control the insect population. These lines or clusters of trees provide brilliant fall color, and, when the leaves fall, a winter mulch.

In making her choices of which trees are worthy, she is a stern judge. To qualify for her forest a tree must have fine structure, form, and habit. Even in its youth, a tree should have grandeur. Its winter presence, outlined against the sky, should be a picture in the landscape. Its foliage must be clear in color in spring, summer, and fall. The tree must be disease-resistant—"tough at heart"—and long-lived. And it should be clothed in gorgeous bark—a coat of many colors.

Marlyn also stresses the importance of balancing the planting of a forest with a varied selection of understory trees and shrubs, those smaller, graceful, flowering plants that enhance the character of a forest. For trees, her choices run to *Halesia carolina,* the silver-bell tree; *Sorbus alnifolia,* the Korean mountain ash; *Oxydendrum arboreum,* the sourwood tree; *Chionanthus virginicus,* the white fringe tree; *Amelanchier laevis,* the Juneberry shad, "whose berries are better than any blueberry you've ever eaten." Favorite shrubs are *Calycanthus floridus,* Carolina allspice; *Aesculus pavia,* red buckeye; *Sambucus racemosa* 'Plumosa Aurea', golden elder; *Caenothus americanus,* New Jersey tea; and *Fothergilla major,* the dwarf alder.

CLOCKWISE: *Platanus occidentalis, Quercus palustrus, Gymnocladus dioica, and Prunus maackii.*

BOTANICAL NAME	COMMON NAME	DESCRIPTION
Acer pseudoplatanus	Sycamore maple	Upright-spreading branches, oval or rounded outline; bark grayish, reddish brown, flaking to expose orange-brown inner bark; foliage dark green
Aesculus glabra	Ohio buckeye	Rounded with branches bending toward the ground, then arching back up at the ends; bark ashy-gray, deeply fissured and plated; foliage bright green, changing to dark green and then pumpkin yellow in the fall
Carpinus caroliniana	American hornbeam	Wide-spreading, flat, or round-topped crown; bark slate gray, irregularly fluted; foliage dark green, orange-yellow in fall
Carya ovata	Shagbark hickory	Straight cylindrical trunk with an oblong crown of ascending and descending branches; bark on old trunks shags into long, flat planes; foliage deep yellow-green in summer, rich yellow and golden brown in fall
Castanea dentata	American chestnut	Massive, wide-spreading branches; deep, broad, rounded crown; gray-brown, strongly ridged bark; serrated, lustrous green foliage. American Chestnut Society distributes seeds of disease-resistant strain
Cercidiphyllum japonicum	Katsura tree	Full, dense, and pyramidal; bark brown and shaggy. Foliage emerges reddish purple, changes to bluish green; fall color yellow to apricot
Cladrastis kentukea (lutea)	American yellowwood	Broad rounded crown of delicate branches; bark gray to light brown; long, pendulous white flowers; bright green foliage, yellow in fall
Fagus sylvatica	European beech	Densely pyramidal, oval or rounded, branches low to the ground; bark smooth and gray, looks like an elephant hide; foliage glossy green or deep maroon-purple, depending on the variety
Fraxinus pennsylvanica 'Marshall's Seedless'	Green ash	Upright-spreading habit; bark grayish brown, furrowed with narrow, interlacing ridges; foliage dark green, yellow in fall
Fraxinus quadrangulata	Blue ash	Slender, straight, tapered trunk with narrow rounded irregular crown; gray bark, often with shaggy scales; foliage dark green, pale yellow in fall
Ginkgo biloba	Ginkgo, Maidenhair tree	Pyramidal when young, wide-spreading massive branches when mature; bark grayish brown ridges with darker furrows; foliage bright green, yellow in fall
Gymnocladus dioica	Kentucky coffee tree	Vertically ascending branches; bark has firm, scaly ridges that curl outward; new foliage pink to purple, changing to dark green
Liriodendron tulipifera	Tulip tree	Oval to rounded with sinuous branches; bark grayish brown with rounded ridges and crevices; foliage bright green, golden yellow in fall
Nyssa sylvatica	Black tupelo	Pyramidal when young, flat or rounded top when mature; dark gray bark with thick irregular ridges; can become scaly; foliage lustrous green, orange-red in fall
Platanus occidentalis	American sycamore	Massive trunk, wide-spreading open crown; white-mottled bark; medium to dark green foliage
Prunus maackii	Amur bird cherry	Rounded, dense branching; cinnamon-brown bark, exfoliates in shaggy masses; dark green foliage; black fruit in fall, persisting through winter
Quercus alba	White oak	Upright or broad-rounded with wide-spreading branches; bark ashy gray, deeply fissured; foliage dark green, deep purplish red in fall
Quercus bicolor	Swamp white oak	Broad with rounded crown; bark grayish to flaky brown with long, flat fissures; foliage dark green, yellow and reddish purple in fall
Quercus macrocarpa	Bur oak	Massive trunk, broad crown of stout branches; grayish brown bark, deeply ridged and furrowed; lustrous dark green foliage, yellow-brown in fall
Quercus muehlenbergii	Chinquapin oak	Open, rounded crown; ashy gray bark, rough and flaky; lustrous yellowish green foliage, yellowish brown in fall
Quercus palustris	Pin oak	Oval-pyramidal form; grayish-brown bark with shallow ridges and furrows; glossy dark green foliage, bronze or red in fall
Quercus rubra	Red oak	Magnificent rounded, open form, often symmetrical; deep brown bark, broken into wide flat-topped edges; lustrous dark green foliage, deep russet red in fall
Quercus velutina	Black oak	Wide-spreading or elongated; almost black, furrowed bark; dark green foliage

SEED SAVIOR

William Woys Weaver
Devon, Pennsylvania

WILLIAM WOYS WEAVER is a keen observer. Promptly at ten o'clock each morning he strides toward his vegetable garden, which stretches across a verdant acre in a series of raised beds in the style of an 1830s *jardin potager*. There, Will records the last twenty-four hours' progress of a vast array of open-pollinated or heirloom vegetables, which he has grown from his personal inventory of seeds—The Roughwood Seed Collection. In the twenty years since he started this garden, Will has cultivated 3,000 different varieties: 95 types of lettuce, 53 different potatoes, 220 rare tomatoes, 83 kinds of garlic, 38 types of corn, 191 peppers, and 268 beans.

Meticulous record keeping is the cornerstone of his approach. Will notes, for example, exactly when a particular potato was planted, when it emerged, when it produced its first flower, when it was

William Woys Weaver

"In the eighteenth century, people looked at plants for their usefulness, and their usefulness was their beauty."

ready to harvest—and how it tastes. He lists the planting date of corn and the moment it came to tassel. Details like those may suggest further experiments, like what pepper he might cross with another. His quest is for new, unusual strains. "Because I am around vegetables all the time, I see characteristics and traits that someone else might not see," he says. On a recent day he was watching a head of lettuce that had thrown a sport. It was an unusually large head, open-leafed and speckled with purple, as though dabbed by a brush dipped in the juice of a plum. That head will be allowed to flower, or bolt. When the plant passes through this unwieldy stage, it is staked and tied until its seeds are dry and ripe for collection. "The process of selection and breeding may give this garden a slightly disheveled look," Will observes, "but I maintain a laboratory, not an ornamental garden."

Food historian, writer, lecturer, cook, gardener, and guardian of heirloom vegetable strains, Will is a man who wears many hats, "but all are related." His 1997 *Heirloom Vegetable Gardening* is a monumental 400-page compendium of antique plants that documents the history and the sociology of their development and provides instruction on the best growing practices. Amid this prodigious research, Will slipped in irresistible recipes with names like Angel Locks (slivered red carrots napped with a sugar syrup) and Sellerie-Salat (celeriac salad). He is, after all, a superb chef. The year 2000 marked the publication of Will's two books: *Sauer's Herbal Cures,* his study of America's first herbal written by Christopher Sauer in the eighteenth century, and *100 Vegetables and Where They Came From.* "I write books to get chefs revved up about these plants. I'm the missionary encouraging people to grow them."

PREVIOUS PAGE, RIGHT: **Will's sentimental attachment to Musselburgh leek (***Allium ampeloprasum***), originally from Scotland, harks back to his great-grandmother's garden. He still uses her recipe for leek, fig, and fennel root pie. THIS PAGE,** BELOW: **A straight brick path leads from Will's house, past the "essential" 60-foot-long greenhouse, to the vegetable garden, which is contained by an ornamental lattice**

fence. OPPOSITE: **The Blue Shackamaxon Bean (***Phaseolus vulgaris***), preserved by Quaker farmers of southeastern Pennsylvania, is said to have been cultivated by the Lenape as early as the 1700s.**

Plants bring stories. Also a writer of mystery fiction, Will is a compelling raconteur. He tells of the Trail of Tears Bean, which members of the Cherokee Nation carried on their forced march from North Carolina to Oklahoma during the winter of 1838–1839; it remains a symbol of their struggle for survival and identity. The diminutive cannonball cabbage, which Will believes to be the best cabbage for small gardens, was introduced in 1868 by James H. Gregory of Marblehead, Massachusetts, but it probably originated in Copenhagen.

Plants' picturesque names—*Couve tronchuda* (Portugal cabbage), Brauner Trotzkopf Lettuce, *Schimmeig stoo* (a striped yellow and orange tomato)—roll off Will's tongue in

TOP: **The gorgeous** *Schimmeig stoo* **tomato is hollow inside, making it perfect for stuffing, Will notes.** ABOVE: **The beans displayed decoratively in an old wooden bowl are Corossnanny Pole (a Pennsylvania Dutch variety), Flagg Pole (an Iroquois bean), Jackson Wonder Bush Lima (dating from 1888), and Speckled Saba (dating from before 1700).**

flawless enunciation, since he speaks German, French, Italian, and Spanish. He can read Greek, "but I simplify that by translating the Greek into Latin," he says.

Will travels widely, from England to Cyprus, in search of seeds. He trades with like-minded preservationists around the world, often using his own plants, like the Roughwood golden plum tomato, proven to be drought-resistant. From Botswana he procured a ground-nut that contains all the nutrients of a perfect food; from Nicaragua he acquired a fiery pepper; and he found a summer-blooming poinsettia from Mexico.

He maintains a daunting amount of data on each variety. All of his varieties are numbered, most are named. A number is always recorded on a plant's name label in the garden; when punched in on his computer, a flood of information about that plant, from history to harvest, is released. The repeated cycle of saving seeds, of replanting and observing, of stabilizing a variety takes ten to fifteen years. He notes ruefully, "I'd have to be Methuselah to see all the fruits of my labors."

Will is a life member of the Seed Saver's Exchange, an organization dedicated to preserving the world's heirloom vegetables. He consults for organizations like the Center for Food, Wine and the Arts in Napa Valley, and Pennsbury Manor in Bucks County, identifying historically correct strains and providing the seeds that are grown in those gardens. A rare Native American corn, 'Delaware India Blue', is now being cultivated in Old Salem, North Carolina. "Two hundred plants ensure genetic stability," Will notes. "Obviously I cannot grow that many of one variety here, so I enlist the aid of organizations that have the space—and the willingness—to grow them for me.

"Heirloom vegetables taste better, and for that reason alone many gardeners seek and grow them, but it is very important to remember," Will says, "that work like this could save future generations from famine." As commercial seed companies are bought by chemical and petroleum conglomerates, vegetable hybrids are bred to be dependent on their fertilizers and pesticides. An unpredicted blight or disease could wipe out crops around the world. He cites the Irish potato famine of the 1840s and the devastation of the corn crop in the American South in the 1970s. When diversity is maintained within a species, a disease that strikes one variety will not necessarily attack another.

Lining every surface in his dining room, pantry, and kitchen are containers of seeds. One aspect of Will's testing program is determining how long seeds remain viable, and he does not grow every variety every year. The frequency depends on a particular variety's seed viability in storage. He purchased a cache of glass pickle jars from a factory that was closing. However, glass allows light to pass through it, and so he is in the process of changing his storage system to square brown plastic containers designed for medical use. A seed room in the cellar is kept at the same temperature year round, and Will plans to install a new refrigeration system, where the humidity will be as low as possible and the temperature will remain at 40°F. This will be particularly convenient as the potato collection increases and needs larger winter storage quarters.

In 1979, Will purchased his gracious three-story Federal-style home, which is on the

OPPOSITE, TOP RIGHT: **Pipián de nicaragua pumpkin** (*Cucurbita moschata*) **fills a bed with its decorative speckled foliage.** BELOW LEFT AND RIGHT: **Will practices vertical planting, constructing teepees of bamboo for the Blue Shackamaxon Bean and hops. Even more creatively, "I often use one plant as the structural support for another," he says, indicating pole beans growing up cornstalks.**

TOP: **Painted pumpkin orange, its original color, Will's house dominates its surroundings, even as the paint mellows over time.**
ABOVE: **Harvest in a basket: Turkish Orange eggplants, Chiltoma Larga peppers, Yellow Peach tomato, Neon eggplant, large Red and Brown Flesh tomatoes.**
RIGHT: **Will's enclosed garden with rectilinear raised beds is based on the traditional quadrant style. He believes these design principles maximize the growing areas, both vertically and horizontally, and economize on the workload.**

National Register of Historic Places. Since it was built in 1805, it has seen several incarnations, from being the Lamb Tavern to its years as a farm. "A bit worn around the edges" is the way Will describes the house's condition when he bought it, but even in that state the twenty-eight-room house, with 13-foot ceilings on the ground floor and eight fireplaces, "had great class." Will, who has a degree in architecture from the University of Virginia, undertook an extensive restoration. In the spirit of the era of the house, Will amassed an extensive collection of antique kitchen implements. "I could reconstruct an 1823 kitchen right down to the wooden clothespins," he says.

Will designed his raised beds using aerial photographs that showed the shadow outlines of the original eighteenth-century vegetable garden. He touts the advantages of this arrangement: good drainage, easily amendable, no compaction of the soil, and "you can crowd more

plants in than if the beds are on the ground." Built of 1-by-12-inch cedar boards held in place by sturdy 2-by-4 stakes, the beds vary in size from 4-by-4 feet to as large as 16-by-16 feet. His mistake, he says, was to make the paths too narrow—only 2 feet wide. "When you lay out your paths," he advises, "consider the width of a large wheelbarrow." For flexibility in planting, each large bed is separated into smaller sections, using the shape of a square as both a design element and a practical division. To ensure healthy plants, Will rotates crops on a three- to five-year plan. In addition, he uses many sections of the beds progressively throughout the season. One square may first hold potatoes, then bush beans, followed by winter lettuce.

Flowers mixed with vegetables serve as vibrant punctuation points at the corners of the beds. Many have assigned tasks. Amaranth, for example, lures the potato beetles and slugs away from the potatoes; they like amaranth better. Other delicacies divert bumblebees from pollinating peppers; the bumbles prefer cleomes, cosmos, zinneas, and tithonias. Ideas for mixing flowers and vegetables abound, like employing sunflowers and corn as supports for pole beans.

The garden is 100 percent organic. Will rarely uses manure, and if he does, it is well-rotted horse manure. Instead, he maintains a routine of composting, rotating plant material through three bins, grinding it each time it is moved to the next bin. In the spring he adds rock phosphate and gypsum, which is also used in making plaster of Paris. The gypsum does not change the chemistry of the soil, but rather its molecular composition, unbinding the clay, making it looser. Will often puts vegetable kitchen scraps right into the beds to decompose in situ. A local Italian restaurant saves oyster shells and clamshells, which Will deposits in the garden to add calcium to the soil. For feeding plants, he uses fish emulsion.

To deter rabbits, squirrels, and deer, Will dangles CDs on strings from bamboo stakes. As the discs twirl in the wind they send beams of sun- or moonlight bouncing through the garden.

The location of the vegetable garden, a slightly sloping southwest-facing arena, is ideal. "I

LEFT: **A gate leads into the walled garden, where Will is installing cordoned fruit trees on the stone walls.**
BELOW: **For pure color, thirty different dahlias come into the garden each spring from their winter hibernation in the greenhouse. Will professes, "I've always been a dahlia man." Two favorites are the salmon-tinged Nutley Surprise and the Orange Julian.**

love Pennsylvania," Will says. "I can grow anything that can grow in Maine or North Carolina here. We're supposed to be Zone 6, but this warm side of the hill behind us is really 7A. If I don't get a frost by October 13, then I don't get it until Thanksgiving. That's been as predictable as arthritis since about 1900."

House and gardens, the growing of ingredients, and the preparation and pleasure of food are a seamless continuum in Will's world. To the east of the house a walled garden, which used to hold ornamental plants, is under renovation. Vegetables and fruit are moving in. Will is planting cordoned apple trees along its 10-foot-high stone walls. Close to the front door a small, enclosed medicinal herb garden is a nod to a monastery cloister.

Will says he came to his passion genetically—his family arrived in Pennsylvania thirteen generations ago to work the earth. "My grandfather was a great influence; he endowed me with a green thumb," he says of the man who taught him to garden. "I still grow many of my grandfather's plants, from his rhubarb to his comfrey."

SUPER SPUDS
Heirloom Potatoes

"POTATOES ARE my soul food," says Will Weaver, and to prove it he has grown more than ninety different varieties—all heirlooms. "With potatoes, as with apples, the tremendous variations in color, texture, and taste are a great delight to the gardener and the cook."

Each year, as Will harvests his potato crops, he selects as seed potatoes the finest specimens of each variety. He stores them at 40°F in labeled and stacked organic

from a potato and plant that part, a method Will follows only for his larger potatoes, like 'All Red'. Since he favors many egg-size potatoes, he plants those smaller seed potatoes whole. He plants each variety—"twenty-four to thirty-six tubers, multiples of twelve, as that's what the egg cartons hold"—in its own small patch, approximately 6 to 8 feet square. "I'm looking for variety, not quantity." He places them about a foot apart in

holes at least 6 to 8 inches deep, 10 inches if it is a big-tuber variety, like 'All Red' or 'All Blue'. They are spaced 8 to 14 inches apart on all sides, again depending on the size. "Give them plenty of room," Will advises. "Crowding reduces harvest yields."

Will feeds his entire vegetable garden with his own compost. Animal manure, he says, can introduce scab into the soil, and once present, it is very hard to eliminate. He does not mound the soil;

LEFT: Cow Horn, All Red, Catriona, Early Rose, and All Blue potatoes. RIGHT: A Shetland Blue Eye potato in flower.

egg cartons that have no open slits; thus the tubers remain in total darkness and are prevented from drying out during the winter months. Will checks his cache periodically to weed out any potatoes that have gone bad.

Potatoes, like tomatoes, appreciate soil that is rich, loamy, loose, and slightly acid. He provides potassium in the form of rock phosphate. He rotates his potatoes, as is his routine with all vegetables in his garden. Will begins to plant in mid-March and continues through mid-April. "Each potato has its own clock, both for breaking dormancy and for its growing cycle. When they turn a bit green and begin to bud, the potato is ready to plant." He forces potatoes in his greenhouse, although some will bud while still refrigerated. Common practice is to cut a section with a budded eye

rather, he mulches his potatoes with salt hay. The mulch performs multiple duties: it discourages weeds; it keeps the plants cool in hot weather and prevents them from drying out; and it deters slugs. To control the Colorado potato beetle, Will sprays with insecticidal soap. Applying it early can kill the grubs, and from then on Will sprays on a weekly basis. For the rare infestation, he sparingly scatters wood ash around the plants, which just adds more potassium to the soil. Blight, wilt, and other viral diseases are a greater threat in an organic garden. At the first sign of those problems, Will advises destroying the plants by burning them in a location removed from the garden.

Potatoes are classified as early, midseason, or late—generally from 90 to 120 days, although a few take 150 days. "Potatoes are easy," says Will. "When the tops—the foliage—dies, they tell you, 'I'm done, I'm ready, dig me.'"

POTATO
(*Solanum tuberosum*)

VARIETY NAME	DESCRIPTION
'All Blue'	Blue-black skin, white band under skin, center solid blue or white with blue veining; remains blue after cooking; earthy potato-chip flavor; blue-lilac flowers, plants 27 to 28 inches tall
'All Red'	Tubers 4½ to 5 inches long, 2½ inches wide; plants 18 to 22 inches tall; flowers lilac to violet; plants not bothered by dry conditions
'Arran Victory'	Pale violet skin when freshly dug, white flesh; white flower; weak 24-inch vines; prefers cool, moist ground
'Bliss's Triumph'	Good boiling potato when cooked in the skins; small and somewhat sweeter than most potatoes; white flowers, large leaves on robust plants
'Catriona'	Smooth tan tubers, shaped like a flat kidney bean; deep violet eyes with occasional violet patches on skin; pale yellow flesh; pale lilac flowers; plants 32 to 33 inches tall
'Chile Ancud'	Pale violet skin similar to 'Arran Victory', but with brown overtones and elongated shape; white flowers; plants 16 inches tall; prefers sandy soil and moist conditions
'Cow Horn'	Purple skin, off-white flesh; tubers are curved, bent with deep lumpy eyes; fine baking potato; white flowers; plants 27 to 28 inches tall
'Cups'	Tuber resembles 'The Lumper' but ripens pink in storage; eyes turn pink; white flesh; flowers white to pale pink; plants 20 to 22 inches tall, rambles on ground
'Duke of York'	Yellow flesh and skin; best as a new potato, as it gets more floury as it matures in storage; tender and buttery, when boiled; skin is covered with small flakes; white flowers; low floppy plants; does not overwinter well in the ground for fall planting
'Early Rose'	Pink blush to skin, waxy; prefers loose, sandy loam; white flowers are normally sterile; plants about 21 inches tall
'Garnet Chili'	Small, round with rose skin; good for boiling and for salads; white flower; plants 16 inches tall; for large tubers, leave in the ground as long as possible
'La Ratte d'Ardeche'	Flavor more intense when served cool or cold; lilac-pink flowers; plants 14 inches tall
'The Lumper'	Tubers misshapen, lumpy, smooth tan-colored skin; flesh white; white flower, usually infertile; plants 22 to 24 inches; does not thrive in sandy soils
'Negresse' (*Solanum ajanhuiri*)	Skin nearly black, dark purple-violet firm flesh, juice like ink when first cut; flowers snowy white; lanky plants 20 to 22 inches tall
'New England Blue'	Tuber is long and sometimes branching like a ginger root; skin is rose-violet or lilac; pale white flower tinged with violet; perhaps not a *tuberosum*; plants 24 to 30 inches tall
'Peach Blow'	Mealy, excellent boiled or steamed, rich potato flavor; flower pale pink; plants about 24 inches tall
'Peruvian Purple'	Small fingerling type; purple-black skin, purple marbled flesh; most tubers smaller than a thumb; white flower; plants 12 to 14 inches tall
'Roseval'	Fingerling type; smooth dark-red skin, oval, yellow flesh; good for boiling, excellent for potato salad; complex flavor holds up well after cooking; flowers white tinged with pink; tall, spindly plants; plant as early as possible in Pennsylvania; requires watering to develop properly
'Snowflake'	White, flaky flesh; light green leaves that are large and pointed; white flower; can be planted deep for overwintering for a June harvest the following season; best when planted at the end of May in many areas; plants 24 inches tall
'White Beauty of Hebron'	Yellow-white skin; white flowers; medium early; plants 22 inches tall
'The Yam'	White flesh; tubers develop large round bud on the root end, resembling a nipple; showy white clusters of flowers; plants 20 to 22 inches

SUBLIME SIMPLICITY

Neville Frierson Bryan
Lake Bluff, Illinois

NEVILLE BRYAN knows when to stop. Whether in the choice of an individual ornament, like an flawless eighteenth-century urn, or in the dramatic repetition of a single plant—a vast sweep of *Hosta sieboldiana* var. *elegans* at the edge of the lawn, for instance—Neville speaks eloquently by saying little.

She and her husband, John, a corporate executive, garden on a spectacular 150-acre property high on a bluff overlooking Lake Michigan, where they have created a series of interconnected gardens in harmony with a larger landscape. With buildings that had eluded updating and land that retained the character of its use as an early-twentieth-century farm, the property provided them with an unspoiled piece of American architectural and gardening history, two interests that had long been in their blood.

Neville Frierson Bryan

"Our goal is a seamless integration of buildings and gardens."

Neville grew up in Arkansas and John in Mississippi; the couple met at Rhodes College in Tennessee. John chose the University of Virginia for his graduate studies in business, because of his avocation, a love for architecture and an admiration for Thomas Jefferson. Today he considers himself an amateur architect. The couple settled in West Point, Mississippi, John's hometown, where he took over his family-owned meat-packing business. "We always had gardens around our home," Neville says, "and I never thought we would live anywhere but Mississippi." However, in 1968 John merged his family's company with Consolidated Food Corporation, now the Sara Lee Corporation. The couple, who by that time had four children, moved to Kenilworth, on Chicago's North Shore.

The joining of the Bryans and their current property is an ideal marriage. Neville and John have researched the estate's history, assembling a comprehensive collection of period records, both architectural and horticultural, from which they draw as they restore the property—and integrate their own understated twenty-first-century style into the property's distinguished lineage.

In 1911 Grace Durand, a forward-thinking woman from a prominent Lake Forest family, commissioned Solomon Beman to design a dairy farm. As John observes, "Mrs. Durand was an anomaly; what she did was highly unusual at the time." The barns and silos in the Arts and Crafts style were sited on a slight rise set back from the road. But considerable land still remained between the farm and the lake. In 1926 eleven acres between the farm and the water were sold to William McCormick Blair, great-nephew of Cyrus McCormick, the inventor of the reaper. Blair, an investment banker, planned to build a summer home.

In 1926 the renowned Chicago architect David Adler was commissioned to design the house. Adler took a detour from his signature style, which was more symmetrical and formal in nature. This house, while a sprawling 8,000 feet, was modeled on the Cape Cod cottage— "a grand house in an ungrand style, similar to those in Newport or on the Maine coast," observes John. Although the house has an informal atmosphere, Adler lavished typical attention to detail on every inch, from paneling to porch.

The two properties, the Blair summer cottage and the Durand dairy farm, were reunited in the 1950s, and the Bryans purchased the estate in 1984. Its escape from modernization

PREVIOUS PAGES: **Whether meticulously pruning an espaliered euonymus against the stone wall of the house or placing a single bench between the house and a view of Lake Michigan, Neville Bryan exercises restraint in all her gardening decisions.** THIS PAGE, ABOVE: **Typical of Neville's attention to detail, she commissioned a curved bench for the Rose Garden based on one in an original drawing made by Ellen Biddle Shipman.**

Critical to the architectural
spirit of the garden are the
allées that extend through
gardens and forest, creating
a clearly defined north-
south grid system. Some
terminate in garden orna-
ments; others lead to
entrances of buildings, like
the gracious doorway of the
1928 tennis house or the
classical arcade of
Jeffersonian folly. One skirts
a quiet resting spot with a
John Makepeace bench and
a playhouse with a view of a
distant wildflower meadow.

appealed to their passion for preservation—John is the former chairman of the National Trust Council of the National Trust for Historic Preservation.

The overall property plan also featured a neoclassical garden folly in the form of a miniature Jeffersonian villa, an indoor tennis house in the handsome 1920s style, and a vegetable and fruit garden with a Lord & Burnham greenhouse. The parterre design of the walled garden that graces the front of the house was laid out by Ellen Biddle Shipman, whom many hail as the dean of American women landscape architects; a drawing of her original plan remains in the Bryan collection. Jens Jensen, a revered Midwest landscape architect known for his prairie style, is reputed to have left his imprint as well, although no existing documentation attests to what extent.

The Bryans launched into a full-scale restoration project, including establishing woodworking, pottery, and metalworking workshops on the property. If the Bryans build a gate for a new garden, each part, including the hardware, is created in the workshops. When a lantern was needed to complete the top of a column, a photograph of an onion-shaped one David Adler had designed provided the inspiration; reproductions were crafted in the Bryan metal shop. "We have had to do *everything,*" Neville insists.

By its very nature, the enclosed vegetable and cutting garden has more ebullient planting than the other gardens, but it, too, follows geometric design principles. Even the focal elements, like the rigorously pruned aged pear at the gable end of the potting shed, are conceived to be clean and simple. Neville says, "For me, gardening and editing go hand in hand."

These days an understated white wood fence runs parallel to the road. A subtle sign announces Crab Tree Farm, which is the only remaining farm in Illinois on Lake Michigan. The magnificent barns are restored; every tile on every roof has been renewed; Hereford cattle and sheep mingle in the pastures, chickens weave between the legs of glistening horses, wheat waves in the fields; the orchards, planted in mathematical grids, are pruned to perfection. Two pristine ponds, surrounded by natural-looking plantings, are guarded by a pair of swans that alternately glide peacefully across the water's still surface and aggressively guard their eggs on their own private island.

The gravel drive, which winds past another enclave of buildings, including the original stables and the caretaker's cottage, leads unexpectedly to an old forest of red and white oak, walnut, and hickory carpeted with native ferns. The Bryans' deep concern for this natural gift is underscored by the fact that 30 acres of their land is designated conserved woodland. The trees are pruned high, and as John says, lifting his eyes to the cathedral of green overhead, "This is as good a forest as exists."

Pruning is a preoccupation in the Bryan gardens. A Bryan grandson once observed, "Papa lives on a farm. He trims his trees; that's why it looks so neat." Every tree—from a single espaliered euonymus on a gabled wall of the house to an ancient pear on the potting shed— receives their studied attention. While the effect appears natural, meticulous grooming is the discipline that affords the gardens their appearance of effortless grace. Considered attention to shape and proportion is the key to such visual pleasure. As they determine every form, from an individual tree's habit to the shape of an 800-foot alleé, the Bryans ask themselves what the eye will perceive and believe. A single tree can be managed to extend across the

BELOW: Boxwood hedges line the parterres, which feature pastel-colored roses for the summer months. A graceful, asymmetrically pruned tree at the far end and the exuberant 'New Dawn' rose draping the wall add elements of tension to the otherwise formal design. OPPOSITE: Neville mixes a myriad of flowers, vegetables, and herbs throughout her vegetable and cutting garden. Again, formal lines prevail, whether they be axial paths; low, crisply

entire end of a garden, and an allée may be tapered from a width of 22 feet at its opening to 11 at its far end to make it appear longer.

The Bryans also stress the importance of transitions between gardens, of harmony between what could be disparate elements. Simply stated, it is impossible to bring the formal plantings, like boxwood, out into the woods; it is much more successful to draw the woodland plants, like ferns, in closer to the house. The Bryans often let nature be their guide. Moss that grows between stones and on the wood shingles inspired the color of the shutters on the house. Many design decisions are based on editing; the Bryans stress that less really is more.

The Ellen Shipman garden, enclosed by the U shape of the house and a low stone wall, is now called the Rose Garden. "She designed it to have every inch filled with perennials—a very labor-intensive garden," says Neville as she pores over the Shipman drawing. Over the years the original garden had disappeared, if indeed it ever was executed exactly like the plan. Neville determined to restore the garden to the plan, including the parterres, the pond and the fountain. "Because of the drawing, we could get the bones exactly the way

clipped hedges of boxwood or germander; the structure of 6-foot-tall fruit cages; or positions of the arbors. An original Lord & Burnham greenhouse provides Neville with her winter headquarters as she experiments with new plants. "After all," she says, "so much of gardening is about discovery."

Ellen Shipman intended, using stone and slate, the materials she specified," she adds.

The parterres are outlined with boxwood. However, the beds planted only with pastel and white roses are a restrained but lush departure from Shipman's scheme. In early spring before the roses bloom the parterres are underplanted with a carpet of lavender-blue pansies. But once the roses begin their summer-long display, the pansies are quickly removed. "Much too much color," says Neville. The deep brown mulch, a complementary background for the roses, is refreshed as needed.

Since Neville is a fine cook, an immediate priority was the reclamation of the vegetable and fruit garden, a 120-by-85-foot enclosure situated to the west of the indoor tennis court. At the center of its east-west axis is a raised stone hexagon featuring an armillary sphere, the single ornament in the garden. Arbors of privet and bittersweet mixed with Boston ivy give the design height and suggest a division of the space into rooms.

Neville incorporated flowers for cutting, in the style of the *Jardin Potager* at Villandry in France, into a new planting program, as she likes each room of the house to contain a fresh bouquet. A couple dozen peonies remain from the original plantings, and Neville notes that

"These old varieties of peonies can live longer than people." She adds new varieties of flowers each year, selected by color schemes she wishes to coordinate in rooms of the house.

The 24-by-60-foot greenhouse, which also includes an orchid room, was in disrepair and had to be restored. "We had to take it apart and put it back together. That's where I spend my winters," says Neville of the place where she nurtures plants and grows annuals and perennials and vegetables from seed. "I grow things I can't get here, like black-eyed peas, lima beans, okra, and turnip greens." A fenced, shelved, and shaded courtyard protects tender plants from the summer's hot sun. On the south side of the greenhouse is an herb garden, featuring abundant quantities of sage, mint, dill, sorrel, chives, rosemary, Italian parsley, and basil.

The garden's design is ordered, efficient, and practical. The herbs are contained by germander hedges, punctuated at the corners by balls of boxwood. Rustic pyramids support tomatoes and nasturtiums. Cold frames—"essential for hardening off the seedlings"—line the exterior north side of the greenhouse. Several 6-foot-high fruit cages contain strawberries, blueberries, and raspberries, their feet blanketed with salt hay. Pea-sticks or iron cages

prevent flowers from flopping. An overhead watering system, with eight heads installed at regular intervals, allows selected portions of the garden to be watered. The garden is enclosed by hedges and, on one side, an apple tree allée.

The apple allée divides the vegetable and cutting garden from the Walled Garden, a ten-year-old Bryan addition. A study in understatement, the plantings are primarily green: a dozen balls of boxwood seem arbitrarily scattered within a bed in which a magnificent lead statue of the Venus de Medici holds court in her bower of yew. She faces Mercury, also made of lead, who stands outside the garden's large wooden gate at the end of an axis line. The interlocking rectilinear shapes of the garden's beds, surrounded by clipped boxwood, were inspired by shapes and patterns in Mondrian paintings. Some beds are planted with masses of a single plant, like alpine lady's mantle, which makes a textural foil for the box balls, or caryopteris, its delicate foliage set off by the deep green of a yew hedge. Other borders are layered, with the shapes of leaves seeming the determining factor for plant choice. Epimedium, bleeding heart, ligularia, and cimicifuga are defined by a background of climbing hydrangea (*Hydrangea petiolaris*), happily draped and blooming on the north

THIS PAGE: **Neville repeatedly speaks of the necessity of enclosure, a design issue she says is often ignored in American gardening. In the Walled Garden one cannot see over or through the walls, providing a sense of separation from the rest of the world that is enhanced by the singular palette of greens and the spare placement of ornaments.** OPPOSITE: **From the edge of the bluff a long series of steps lead down to the Sculpture Garden, which parallels the shore of Lake Michigan. Several hauntingly ambigu-**

ous pieces by sculptor Anna (Muska) Benes, like the Cherry Walk, have been placed in wooded settings. The works seem timeless— a perfect bridge between things ancient and modern.

side of the wall. Native hawthorns stand as subtle accents in the corners of the garden.

Several other garden additions are in the process of being planted or refined: a fern garden, a spring bulb garden, a moss garden, a beach walk, and a sculpture garden. Small, elegant buildings, too, are being erected in the spirit of the original neoclassical garden house: an eighteenth-century English pavilion, a folly bought on a recent trip to England, a stone house, designed as the Bryans imagine David Adler would have done, had he been available for consultation. Paths lead from the more formal inventions out through the picturesque landscape, like the Greensward, celebrated by Frederick Law Olmsted and Calvert Vaux. The farther from the buildings one goes, the more natural the landscape seems. Yet in the hands and eyes of the Bryans, these gardens are not strict imitations of nature. Each is an individual work of art, more powerful because of its aesthetic reserve. The Bryans know when to add nothing.

"The gardens need care and consideration," says Neville, "and I'm always learning more— learning by doing and looking."

A GARDEN FOR CUTTING

A Bouquet in Every Room

NEVILLE BRYAN chooses the plants for her cutting garden by color, shape, and texture—frequently with a particular room and combination of plants in mind. The season begins early, with bulbs, and continues into the late fall, with arrangements often including seed heads and dried flowers. She is particularly interested in foliage that enhances her arrangements, and follows a green theme, preferring flowers like *Zinnia* 'Envy' or the green-flowering tobacco called 'Lime Green'. "I seem to be hooked on green," she confesses.

COMMON NAME	BOTANICAL NAME	DESCRIPTION
Achillea	*Achillea* 'Coronation Gold'	Golden-yellow flower heads; 30–36 inches; perennial
Anagallis, blue pimpernel	*Anagallis linifolia*	Deep blue flowers; 8–12 inches; half-hardy annual
Aquilegia, columbine	*Aquilegia alpina*	Nodding blue flowers, sometimes with white tips; 18–24 inches; perennial
Aquilegia, columbine	*Aquilegia canadensis*	Red and yellow bell-shaped flowers; 24–36 inches; perennial
Aquilegia, granny's bonnet	*Aquilegia vulgaris*	Violet, blue, pink, and white nodding flowers; 36 inches; perennial
Artemesia	*Artemesia ludoviciana* 'Silver Queen'	Lacy gray foliage, spreads from underground runners; keep contained; 30 inches; perennial
Baptisia, false indigo	*Baptisia australis*	Many racemes of blue flowers; to 5 feet; perennial
Bergenia	*Bergenia cordifolia* 'Rotblum'	Pinkish red flower spikes; 18 inches; perennial
Borage	*Borago officinalis*	Deep blue nodding flowers; 24 inches; hardy annual
Bush flower, sapphire flower	*Browallia speciosa*	Blue or white flowers; benefit from pinching; tender annual
Calendula	*Calendula officinalis* 'Pacific'	Double flower heads in apricot-orange, primrose-yellow, cream, and bicolors; 24 inches; annual
Chinese forget-me-not	*Cynoglossum amabile*	Sky-blue flowers; 16 inches; annual or biennial
Clematis	*Clematis recta* 'Purpurea'	Purple young foliage; small star-shaped white flowers; fragrant; 30 inches; needs support
Coreopsis	*Coreopsis grandiflora*	Single 2-inch golden-yellow ray florets; 18–36 inches; perennial
Coreopsis	*Coreopsis tinctoria*	Single 2-inch golden-yellow ray florets; 2–3 feet; hardy annual
Cobaea, cathedral bell, cup-and-saucer vine	*Cobaea scandens*	Flowers 2 inches long, open green, age to purple; climber; perennial; treat as an annual
Celosia, cockscomb	*Celosia argentea* var. *cristata*	Crested velvety coral-orange, cockscomb-type flowers; 25–30 inches; tender annual
Celosia, wheat foxtail	*Celosia spicata* 'Purple Flamingo'	Deep rose-purple plumes; dark green leaves; 12 inches; annual
Coneflower	*Echinacea purpurea*	Purple ray flowers with dark cone; 5 feet; perennial
Cosmos	*Cosmos bipinnatus* 'Early Wonder'	Rose, white, pink, crimson flowers; 4½ feet; tender annual
Craspedia, drumsticks	*Craspedia globosa*	Ball-shaped yellow flowers; 2 feet; annual
Dahlia	*Dalhia*, ssp. 'Yvonne'	Water lily type; pink center, lighter pink outer petals; tubers must be dug and stored indoors for the winter
Gaillardia, blanket flower	*Gaillardia aristata* 'Yellow Sun'	Yellow ray florets; 30 inches; perennial
Geranium	*Geranium* 'Johnson's Blue'	Saucer-shaped blue flowers; 12–18 inches; perennial
Geum	*Geum* 'Mrs. J. Bradshaw'	Semi-double scarlet flowers; 16–24 inches; perennial

Gomphrena, globe amaranth	*Gomphrena* 'Strawberry Fields'	Brilliant globe-like red flowers; 30–32 inches; annual
Helenium, sneezeweed	*Helenium autumnale*	Yellow-orange ray florets; 5 feet; perennial
Heuchera	*Heuchera americana*	Wand-like pink flower; 18 inches; perennial
Japanese anemone	*Amenone × hybrida* 'Robustissima'	Pale pink; 3 feet; perennial
Lady's mantle	*Alchemilla mollis*	Loose cymes of yellowish green flowers; 24 inches; perennial
Lamb's ears	*Stachys byzantina* 'Big Ears'	Woolly gray-green leaves; 12 inches; perennial
Lavender	*Lavandula angustifolia* 'Hidcote'	Dark purple flowers; 24 inches; perennial
Marigold Jubilee hybrid mix	*Tagetes* spp.	Extremely double 4–5 inch yellow flowers; 18–24 inches; annual
Miss Willmott's ghost	*Eryngium giganteum*	Cylindrical steel-blue flowers; 36 inches; perennial
Monarda, bee balm, bergamot	*Monarda didyma*	Bright red, a pass-along plant; 36 inches; perennial
Moonflower	*Ipomoea alba*	Trumpet-shaped white flower, fragrant, evening-blooming, twining; perennial, grown as annual
Nasturtium	*Tropaeolum* spp. 'Moonlight'	Tall climber; cool lemon-yellow flowers; annual
Nepeta	*Nepeta* 'Souvenir d'Andre Chaudron'	Spike-like lavender-blue flowers all summer; 2 feet; perennial
Nicotiana, flowering tobacco	*Nicotiana* 'Lime Green'	Lime-green flowers; 24 inches; annual
Peonies, single and double	*Paeonia lactiflora*	Inherited with the property; shades of pink and white
Phlox	*Phlox*, unknown variety	White and pink flowers; 3 feet; perennial
Poppy, Arctic or Iceland poppy	*Papaver nudicaule*	Bright pink, orange; gold; 12 inches; biennial
Poppy, opium	*Papaver somniferum*	Pale pink flowers on gray foliage; 36 inches; annual
Poppy, Oriental	*Papaver orientale* 'Purple Plum'	Deep purple flowers; 30 inches; perennial
Rosa glauca	*Rosa glauca*	Species rose; arching red stems, gray foliage; single pink flowers
Rose	*Rosa* 'Double Delight'	Pale pink with carmine-red margin and flush on flowers; hybrid tea
Rose	*Rosa* 'Grenada'	Salmon center, bright pink petals; large flowers
Rose	*Rosa* 'Medallion'	Delicate apricot color; large flowers
Rose	*Rosa* 'Mr. Lincoln'	Bright red flowers; fragrant
Rose	*Rosa* 'Olympiad'	Brilliant, unfading red flowers; large flowers
Rose	*Rosa* 'Queen Elizabeth'	Clear, bright pink flowers in clusters
Rose	*Rosa* 'Sunset Celebration'	Apricot-pink flowers
Rose	*Rosa* 'Tournament of Roses'	Large, light pink flowers, deeper on the reverse
Rudbeckia	*Rudbeckia fulgida* var. *sullivantii* 'Goldstrum'	Large golden-yellow flower heads; 24 inches; perennial
Rudbeckia	*Rudbeckia occidentalis* 'Green Goddess'	Flowers 4–5 inches with bright green sepals; central black cone; 3 feet; perennial
Russian sage	*Perovskia atriplicifolia*	Small tubular, violet-blue flowers in tall panicles; 3 feet
Salpiglossis, painted tongue	*Salpiglossis sinuata* 'Royal Hybrid Mix'	Orange, blue, purple flowers; 24 inches; annual
Salpiglossis, painted tongue	*Salpiglossis sinuata* 'Stained Glass'	Orange, pink, purple flowers; 24 inches; annual
Salvia 'Blue Bedder'	*Salvia farinacea* 'Blue Bedder'	Vivid violet-purple spikes; 24 inches; annual
Scabiosa	*Scabiosa caucasica* 'Fama'	Sky-blue flowers; 24 inches; perennial
Scaevola, fairy fanflower annual	*Scaevola aemula* 'Blue Wonder'	Sky-blue flower with white eye; 20 inches; perennial grown as an
Silene, Sweet William, catchfly	*Silene armeria*	Deep carmine-pink flowers; 18 inches; self-seeding annual
Snapdragon	*Antirrhinum majus* 'Cinderella Mix,' 'Rocket Mix'	Wide range of colors; 12–30 inches; annual
Snowdrop anemone	*Anemone sylvestris*	White nodding flowers in spring; 12–20 inches; perennial
Speedwell	*Veronica* 'Sunny Border Blue'	Spikes of tubular, dark violet-blue flowers; 18 inches; perennial
Sunflower	*Helianthus annuus* 'Sun Goddess'	Large velvety golden-yellow petals around chocolate-brown center; 6–8 feet; annual
Sweet pea	*Lathyrus odoratus* 'Eckford's Finest Mix', Captain of the Blues'	Multicolored flowers, climber to 6 feet; annual
Zinnia 'Envy'	*Zinnia elegans* 'Envy'	3–4 inch chartreuse flower; 30–36 inches; annual
Zinnia	*Zinnia* 'Profusion Orange'	Vigorous, bright orange flowers; 12 inches; annual
Zinnia 'Whirligig'	*Zinnia elegans* Whirligig series	Petals marked with contrasting colors: yellow-crimson, red-white, pink-white, bronze-red; 18-24 inches; annual

Acknowledgments

To each of the gardeners represented between the covers of this book I offer my deepest appreciation. I have delighted in our long conversations about the pleasures and challenges of creating your gardens, and I have felt privileged to spend early-morning hours amongst your inspired Edens. You have generously provided your expertise, experience, and good humor, and the gardening world is richer for your gifts. This is your book.

A project like this depends on recommendations from a network of gardeners and members of horticultural institutions across this country. You graciously gave time for lengthy phone conversations, often calling back with additional suggestions and ideas. Through your thoughtful advice an illustrious list of bold, adventuresome American gardeners was assembled. Selecting these twenty-four gardeners as representative was indeed a difficult task.

I wish to thank the American Horticultural Society, the Birmingham Botanical Garden, the Chicago Botanic Garden, the Cloisters of the Metropolitan Museum of Art, the Delaware Center for Horticulture, the Garden Club of America, the Garden Conservancy, the Horticultural Society of New York, the Lady Bird Johnson Wildflower Center, the New York Botanical Garden, the North Carolina State University Arboretum, the Pennsylvania Horticultural Society, the United States Botanical Garden.

I am deeply grateful to: Antonia F. Adezio, Mayde Anderson, Claire Andorka, Tony Avent, Richard Ayres, Ania Baas, Craig Bergmann, Sherran Blair, Margaret Boehm, Diane Botnick, Mary

Boyer, Nancy Brewster, Susan Burd Brogdon, Mary Caldwell, Inga Marie Carmel, Richard Cavender, Diane Clarke, Christine Cook, Thomas Cooper, James David, Denise Delaney, Neil Diboll, Eileen Doolittle, Joe Eck, David J. Ellis, John Fairy, Christine Flannagan, Tres Fromme, Galen Gates, Carlin Good, James Grigsby, Lynne Harrison, Jocelyn Horder, Susanna Imbarguen, Celia Jelley, Tim Johnson, Mark Kane, Sally Kutyla, Geraldine Adamich Laufer, Lee Ziekie Lee, Lisa MacCullough, Lou Marotta, Janet McCaffrey, Muffie Michaelson, Martha Mock, Bill Noble, Sean O'Hearn, Laura Palmer, Molly Peacock, Janet Meakin Poor, Charles Price, Julie Priebe, Hattie Purtell, Judy Quattrochi, Dorothy Raphaely, Joanna Reed, Douglas Ruhren, Felder Rushing, Holly H. Shimizu, Lois Snyderman, Betty Spar, Susan Spears, Timothy Steinhoff, Mary Anne Streeter, Dollie Swenson, Anne Cleves Symmes, Richard G. Turner, Jr., Kent Whealy, Wayne Winterrowd,

Index